ROSS KEMP:
MAFIA
AND
BRITAIN

ROSS KEMP: MAFIA AND BRITAIN

ROSS KEMP

WITH
DAVID ARROWSMITH

C CASSELL

First published in Great Britain in 2024 by Cassell, an imprint of
Octopus Publishing Group Ltd
Carmelite House
50 Victoria Embankment
London EC4Y 0DZ
www.octopusbooks.co.uk

An Hachette UK Company
www.hachette.co.uk

Distributed in the US by
Hachette Book Group
1290 Avenue of the Americas, 4th and 5th Floors, New York, NY 10104

Distributed in Canada by
Canadian Manda Group
664 Annette St., Toronto, Ontario, Canada M6S 2C8

ISBN 978-1-78840-563-8

A CIP catalogue record for this book is available from the British Library.

Typeset in 11.25/18.5pt Miller Text by Jouve (UK), Milton Keynes

Printed and bound in Great Britain.

1 3 5 7 9 10 8 6 4 2

Publisher: Trevor Davies
Editor: Scarlet Furness
Copy Editor: Alison Tulett
Designer: Rachael Shone
Deputy Picture Manager: Jennifer Veall
Indexer: Laurence Errington
Senior Production Manager: Peter Hunt

MIX
Paper | Supporting
responsible forestry
FSC
www.fsc.org   FSC® C104740

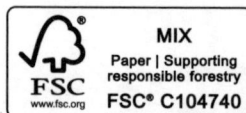

Contents

CONTENTS

The Structure of The Mafia

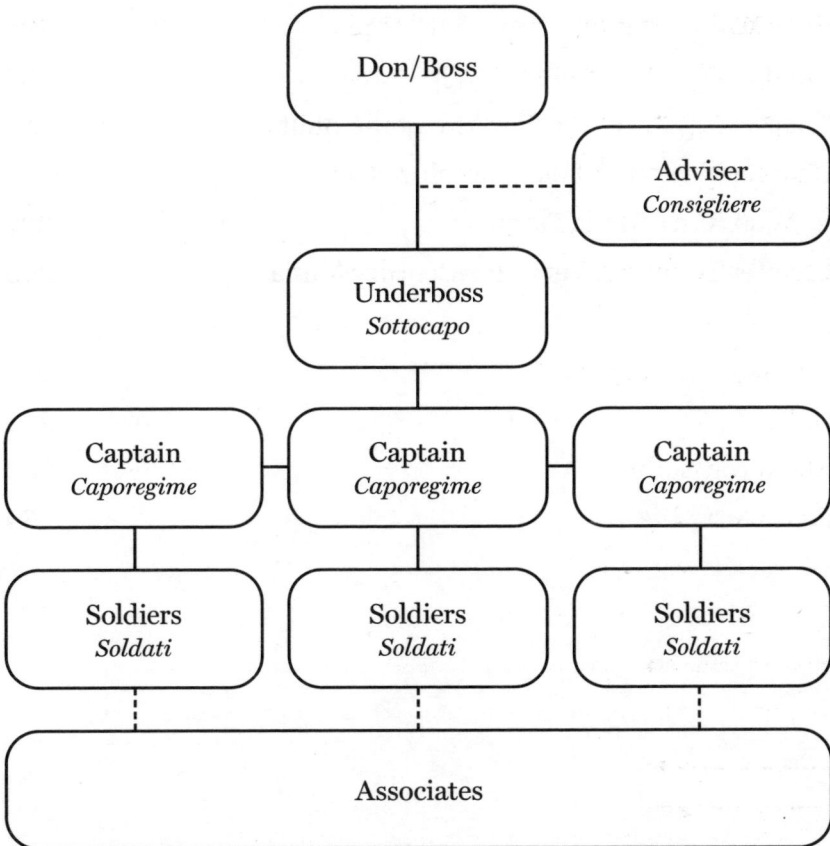

Don/Boss

Adviser
Consigliere

Underboss
Sottocapo

Captain
Caporegime

Captain
Caporegime

Captain
Caporegime

Soldiers
Soldati

Soldiers
Soldati

Soldiers
Soldati

Associates

Introduction

The word 'mafia' quite literally means 'swagger', 'bravado' and 'boldness' in Sicilian.

The Mafia is defined in the dictionary as a secret organization allegedly engaged in smuggling, racketeering, trafficking narcotics and other criminal activities in Italy, the United States and elsewhere. I was about to find out that 'elsewhere' means virtually any other place on planet Earth, including the United Kingdom. My journey into the Mafia's influence in the United Kingdom would take me to the United States, South America, Spain and Italy, but it started and finished in London. Along the way I would encounter some of the most interesting, fearsome, charismatic and fascinating characters I have ever met.

I first watched *The Godfather* as a teenager and was absolutely hooked. I must've watched the movie, parts one, two and three, over 20 times. I became a huge fan of Mario Puzo's work. Later, I was fortunate enough to attend the first London screening of *Goodfellas* and hear Martin Scorsese speak before the film began. For me, *The Sopranos* will always be the best TV series ever made; its genius being in how you sympathize with a character you really shouldn't have sympathy for. I was about to find out that the old cliché is true: that truth really is far stranger than fiction.

I've always been fascinated by the American Mob and their relatives in Sicily and Italy. I have tried to make films about Italian organized crime groups in the past, and while the films weren't bad, I don't think we uncovered as much as we have done in the making of this series. By its very nature, a secret organization is, funnily enough, incredibly secretive! You're also dealing with people who have nothing to gain by engaging with members of the media.

Little did I know then that I would end up talking to two former members of the Italian Mafia, both of whom had lived in the UK – one male, one female. Gennaro Panzuto was a hitman who had continued to kill while living in Preston; he would drive down to Naples at the weekend and then drive back after completing a hit. When I asked him how many people he had killed, he responded with 'too many to remember'. I asked if he could recall their faces, to which he answered, 'not their faces, but I still hear the sound of the bodies hitting the ground'. Marisa Merico, on the other hand, ended up running her father Emilio's Mafia empire in Milan – Emilio being one of the most feared Mafia bosses in Italy. Ridiculously, both she and Gennaro Panzuto had ended up living in Preston unbeknownst to each other!

We also discovered Antonio La Torre, who ran not only restaurants in Aberdeen, but also a Mafia cell. To my knowledge, Antonio is the only member of an Italian organized crime group to be arrested in the UK.

These findings begged the question, why Preston and Aberdeen? Why not London, Birmingham, Liverpool or Manchester? Well, the answer is in the question. Probably the last place law enforcement would look for Mafia activity is Aberdeen or Preston.

I was also surprised to find out that there was an active Mafia cell operating in Woking, Surrey, that imported and exported heroin and laundered money for the Mob.

There is one case, however, that I can remember making the headlines when I first started at drama school in London, in the early 1980s. That was the death of the so-called 'God's Banker', Roberto Calvi. His suicide – or more likely his murder and those responsible for it (the case is still unsolved) – echoes throughout this entire book and is a prime example of just how complex and secretive organized crime groups can be.

One thing that continuously struck me when meeting members of organized crime groups, whether in Europe, the US or South America, was how humbly they lived. The head of the Philly Mob, Angelo Bruno, was assassinated outside his incredibly modest end-of-terrace house, in Philadelphia. It became clear that those who survived often played it low-key and didn't live the highlife. Or, if they did, it happened behind closed doors. Organized crime members who lived openly lavish lifestyles often gained unwanted attention from the authorities, other crime groups, or members of their own family or group. This often led to fatal consequences.

This book is peppered with larger-than-life former gangsters and Mob members, all of whom have no reason to embellish the truth or tell falsehoods. It was absolutely fascinating meeting

Stephen Gillen, who was so well informed about the origin of the Mob's relationship with the UK. In turn, he introduced me to 99-year-old Bobby McKew, a reformed gangster and legend of London's 1960s criminal underworld. Bobby told me how the Krays' involvement in London casinos attracted the attention of the US Mob, who, having been kicked out of Cuba, were keen to diversify their business interests. This information would be backed-up by George 'Cowboy' Martorano, an ex-member of the Philly mob, who explained how at one point he and his father had to literally smuggle Ronnie Kray out of the United States.

Continuing my investigation in the US, I was fascinated to meet ex-Mafia figures straight out of central casting. Although they might have looked and sounded like the characters immortalized by Mario Puzo or Martin Scorsese, these guys were the real thing.

I spoke to 'Crazy Sal Polisi', who worked for both the Gambino and Colombo New York crime families in the 1970s, and who ran with Jimmy 'The Gent' Burke and Henry Hill of *Goodfellas* fame. Sal had no qualms about pulling off a £2 million gold robbery, although he did point out that this was in 1973, at a time when there was no CCTV or DNA testing. He also told me that when he first went to see *The Godfather* at the cinema, he and his fellow gangsters later celebrated by stealing a truck load of cigarettes.

Then there's Anthony Ruggiano Jr., whose father had been sent to Miami by the Gambino family at the beginning of the cocaine boom in the early 1980s. I couldn't help looking at Anthony and thinking of *The Sopranos*. It was his look, his manner and the casual way he talked about the violence in his past.

And Dominick Cicale, a captain in the Genovese family. Again, incredibly charismatic, but a double murderer and take-down merchant. Stealing from drug dealers may have been dangerous, but it earned him millions of dollars a year (and a long term in prison). He eventually turned state's evidence, as did most of my interviewees, in return for a shorter sentence. He knew that the evidence he gave had put some of his closest friends in prison, and he was under no illusion that they would come looking for him when they were eventually released, to seek revenge. His attitude was simply, let them come.

In Colombia I met up with Fernando Rodríguez, the son of Gilberto Rodríguez (the chess player who masterminded, alongside his brother, the biggest cocaine empire that the world has ever seen). To quote American journalist Ron Chepesiuk, if Pablo Escobar was the Henry Ford of the cocaine trade, then the Rodríguez brothers were the McDonald's – they globalized it. Ron also introduced me to the 'British king of cocaine', Jesus Ruiz-Henao, who had the first ever £1 billion UK cartel.

In Spain, I learned how old-time gangsters got involved with the Mafia while trying to muscle in on the cocaine trade. And how a bloody drugs war had brought about a crackdown.

I discovered how the Italian financial police, despite their best efforts, can't prevent an estimated 70 million grams of cocaine being smuggled through a southern port in the south of the country each year. I met an ex-member of the Neapolitan Mafia who was making so much money from cocaine profits he bought a Ducati motorcycle each morning and gave it away each night. Well, at least according to him!

Back in the UK and back in Preston (where else?), a meeting with a former Mafia boss would give us a lead that would possibly reveal the identity of the individual who murdered 'God's Banker'.

After travelling to all those countries, what did I actually learn?

Most of my interviewees were *Pentito* or *Pentiti*, 'the penitent' – those who have collaborated with the justice system in return for their freedom. The one thing that struck me was that most of them seemed to regret their Mafia involvement. Some of the people I met had chosen the life of organized crime. For many, however, it was the life that they were born into, not one they had chosen for themselves. There was always an element of sadness and regret when I left each interview.

The Mafia and organized crime groups have always found a way to make money. It is ultimately about the business.

To quote Nucky Johnson, who ran Atlantic City in the 1920s, 'we have whiskey, wine, women and song. I won't deny it, I won't apologize for it and if people didn't want it, then it wouldn't be profitable. And the fact that they do exist, proves to me that people want it.' People want what the Mafia supply, no matter if those things are illegal. Be it alcohol during Prohibition, gambling before it was legal, or narcotics and money laundering today.

Maybe the Mafia's greatest strength is its ability to remain one step ahead of the authorities, becoming less and less visible in the process. If they are operating here in the UK, then one thing is for sure – detecting them is getting harder and harder.

PART ONE

Chapter One

Roberto Calvi – A Message from The Mafia

———

The Mafia. One of the world's oldest, and deadliest, organized crime groups. Originally from Italy, their expansion into the USA in the 20th century and the creation of the American 'Mob' made them synonymous with organized crime across the globe. Thanks to countless films and TV series, from *The Godfather* to *The Sopranos*, the word 'mafia' alone is enough to conjure up images of racketeering, smuggling, guns, drugs and death. But how much do we really know about the Mafia. How far do their tentacles spread? Could they even have reached the shores of Britain?

Today the term 'mafia' is used very generically for a range of organized crime groups. But the original Italian 'mafias' were not one single organization. Then, as now, each different Italian mafia was linked to a different region. The Cosa Nostra is considered the oldest, and originated in rural Sicily, where groups of locals were empowered by their landlords to control the peasantry. In contrast, the Camorra are very much an urban invention and sprang up in the city of Naples, allegedly growing out of alliances formed in the city's prisons. These, and various other mafia groups, coalesced and grew following the Risorgimento – the mid-19th-century movement for the unification of Italy that led to the creation of the Kingdom of Italy in 1861. From this moment on the various Italian mafia groups expanded and increased their power and influence. However, the law making 'Mafia association' – being a member of a mafia group – illegal was only passed in Italy in 1982. Before then, just being part of a mafia was not a crime. And no such law exists in the UK at all.

When I first embarked on this journey to explore the extent of the Mafia's relationship with Britain, I had no idea where the leads I might uncover during my investigation would take me. Nothing could have prepared me for what was to come. It all began when I started looking into one of the most high profile and intriguing stories of the early 1980s: the death, in London, of an Italian man by the name of Roberto Calvi. . .

On 18 June 1982 I was just weeks away from turning 18. On that day, especially as my dad was a detective superintendent in the Metropolitan Police, a breaking and high-profile news story caught my attention. A man had been found dead, hanging underneath a bridge in Central London. But it was only more than 40 years later that I was finally given the opportunity to investigate the significance of the death of Roberto Calvi.

A young postal clerk on his way to work had found a corpse hanging from scaffolding beneath Blackfriars Bridge, one of the capital's key crossings, spanning the River Thames and connecting the City of London on the north bank with the borough of Southwark to the south. He had immediately alerted the police. They discovered the body of a well-dressed man, clean-shaven, wearing smart leather shoes and with his dark grey suit jacket still buttoned up over his white waistcoat and blue-striped shirt. An orange rope, tied in a lover's knot around his neck, held him suspended to the temporary scaffolding that had been erected beneath one of the wrought-iron arches of the bridge. A search of the body uncovered a wallet containing a mix of currency amounting to a total value of around £10,000. He was wearing neither a belt nor a tie, and his expensive wristwatch – perhaps a Patek Philippe – was stopped, reading 1:52am. Even more curiously, five bricks, weighing around 12 pounds, were also found inside his clothing. The initial autopsy revealed he had been dead for only two to six hours when he was discovered. Soon the man was identified, and the story took a sinister turn. This was none other than Roberto Calvi, the head of a large private Italian bank with connections to the Vatican and many of the most famous, powerful and dangerous people in Italy. The City of London Police investigation deemed his death a suicide, and on 23 July 1982 an inquest jury agreed and ruled that Calvi had killed himself. Case closed.

Calvi's widow and son were adamant he had been killed by the Italian Mafia. In 1983 a second inquest returned an 'open' verdict – but it was only much later, nearly two decades in fact, in October 2002, that a new Italian-led investigation uncovered more details, after exhuming the victim's body, that pointed to murder. Their new forensic analysis revealed that the neck injuries Calvi had suffered were inconsistent with those typically caused by suicide by hanging, or indeed by hanging in general. They also discovered that his hands had never touched the bricks found on his body. The Italian and British authorities together attempted to piece together Calvi's final movements. They believed he had left his flat in Chelsea at around 9pm, and enjoyed an Italian meal before boarding a boat on the north bank of the River Thames for what he thought would be an enjoyable late-evening pleasure cruise. Here an assassin snuck up behind him and looped the orange rope around his neck. The killer pulled hard on the cord, lifting his victim off his feet, and garrotted him. Calvi struggled, and his flailing legs caused deep scrapes in the soles of his shoes from the boat's hard deck, but his resistance was futile, he was strangled to death. Investigators worked out that the killer had brought the banker's body to Blackfriars Bridge at just after midnight on 18 June. The orange rope had been tied into a lover's knot to hold the body fast (the knot tightens under pressure), the corpse weighed down with the bricks and allowed to sink below the level of the river as it was high tide. As the tide retreated in the early hours of the morning, the body of Roberto Calvi was gradually revealed to the world.

Thanks to these findings it eventually became clear that this was no suicide, this was no ordinary man, and this was no ordinary murder. Was this, in fact, a murder designed to look like a suicide? Up until that day in 1982 there had been no indication that the Mafia were operating in Britain. If they were, this was a shocking way to announce the fact to the world.

It was this idea – that the Mafia could have been secretly operating within Britain long before the murder of Roberto Calvi – that drove my investigation. What was their relationship with the UK, and what made them feel the need to break cover with this shocking and very public murder? In search of answers, I travelled to the scene of the crime to meet a man who might have some information.

Peter Bleksley was a Metropolitan Police detective in 1982. As we walked along the foreshore of the Thames, Peter wrapped up against the morning breeze in a tan trench coat and looking every inch the retired detective, he talked me through his investigation. He could remember the reports of Calvi's body having been found hanging beneath the bridge that now loomed in the distance as if it was yesterday. It became clear from Peter's account that, despite the initial findings to the contrary, and based on the evidence he had heard and been privy to, he had quickly formed the opinion that this could have been murder. Calvi was 62, a touch overweight and far from in his physical prime. He would have had to climb over the edge of the bridge and navigate his way down and across the complex scaffolding beneath – in Peter's words, 'almost like an acrobat' – only to then tie one end of a rope to the bridge and the other in a noose around his neck and jump, his pockets weighed down with bricks, into the river. Straight away, Peter's first thought had been that this must be murder.

Peter told me that the cash found on Calvi's body was comprised of a mix of currencies including Italian lira and Swiss francs. He also had on his person a passport in the name of Gian Roberto

Calvini. The authorities soon discovered that the passport was a forgery, and that the body was actually that of Roberto Calvi, the chairman of the Banco Ambrosiano, Italy's biggest private bank and one that held significant cash reserves belonging to the Vatican. The dead man was none other than *Il Banchiere di Dio*: God's Banker.

Born in Milan in 1920, Roberto Calvi had banking in his blood – his father was the manager of the Banco Commerciale Italiano, one of the country's biggest banks. When the Second World War ended, the young Calvi joined his father there – but just a couple of years later, in 1947, he left to join Banco Ambrosiano. At the time it was Italy's second biggest bank. Founded in Milan in 1896 by a Catholic lawyer, and named after St Ambrose – the 4th-century archbishop of the city – it was an avowedly Catholic bank that became known as the 'priests' bank'. At one point the bank even required any prospective depositor to first provide a certificate to prove they had been baptized. One of Banco Ambrosiano's chairmen was Franco Ratti – who was the nephew of Pope Pius XI, who became the first sovereign of the Vatican City State upon its creation in 1929.

By the 1960s Roberto Calvi had risen to the post of deputy chairman, and the bank was busy expanding its business – including opening a holding company in Luxembourg in 1963. In 1971 Calvi was made general manager, and by 1975 he had been appointed as chairman. Under Calvi's watch Banco Ambrosiano continued to diversify its investments and interests, with an increasingly political and religious agenda. Off-shore companies were created in the Bahamas and South America, and funds were made available to help finance Italy's biggest newspaper, the *Corriere della Sera*. Calvi also formed a close relationship with American Archbishop Paul Casimir Marcinkus. Marcinkus was the president of the *Istituto per le Opere di Religione* – the Institute for the Works of Religion. The more common name for this organization? The Vatican Bank.

Calvi used Banco Ambrosiano's labyrinthine network of overseas banks and companies to move money out of Italy, to inflate share prices and to secure massive unsecured loans. But in 1978, the Banca d'Italia (Bank of Italy) produced a report on Ambrosiano that predicted future disaster. A criminal investigation was opened. On 29 January 1979 the investigating Milanese magistrate, Emilio Alessandrini, was shot dead on his way to the city's Palace of Justice. He had also been responsible for several high-profile prosecutions of left-wing terrorists for attacks carried out during Italy's ongoing 'Years of Lead' – the violent battle between far-left and far-right groups that had broken out in the late 1960s. It was one of these left-wing terrorist groups, Prima Linea, who were responsible for Alessandrini's assassination. The Bank of Italy official who had overseen the inspection of Ambrosiano, Mario Sarcinelli, was arrested and imprisoned – before being released and eventually completely exonerated.

As we stood in the shadows beneath Blackfriars Bridge, Peter shared another key piece of his investigation with me. As he had dug further into the victim's background he had uncovered another major Italian organization with whom the dead man had links: the Mafia. Calvi was a member of an illegal masonic lodge known as

Propaganda Due, often shortened to 'P2'. Founded in 1877 under the original name of Propaganda Massonica, but suspended in 1976 by the organization that oversaw the masonic lodges of Italy, the Grand Orient of Italy (GOI), P2 were nevertheless believed to have been involved in aspects of the Years of Lead, and there were also rumours that they were behind the arrest of Sarcinelli. P2 also had strong links to the Italian Mafia. And the nickname of the members of this shadowy masonic brotherhood? *'Fratelli neri'* – they were literally the 'black friars', and would wear black cloaks to their secret meetings.

Propaganda Due fell under the auspices of the Grand Orient of Italy, the country's 'grand lodge', founded in 1805 when Italy was under the control of Napoleon. The European masonic orders in the 19th century were very much based on the French model, and Italy was no exception. From 1901 to 1985 the Grand Orient of Italy was based at the Palazzo Giustiniani in Rome. The historic fraternal organization known as Freemasonry had its roots in the 14th century, in the guilds of stonemasons – if not even further back than that, with the Knights Templar. It had grown and spread in the 17th century and become increasingly structured and organized in the 18th and 19th centuries. This was an ancient and global organization. And so, despite being suppressed by Benito Mussolini in 1925, the Freemasons of Italy were able to survive and then expand again following the end of the Second World War.

In 1966 Propaganda Massonica renamed itself Propaganda Due. That same year a new member joined the lodge – Licio Gelli. Gelli was a former Italian 'Blackshirt' – the paramilitary wing of

Mussolini's Fascist Party – who had fought in support of General Franco's fascist rebellion in the Spanish Civil War in the late 1930s, and acted as a liaison officer between Mussolini's government and the powers of Nazi Germany during the Second World War. After the war he had fled to Argentina, accused of torture. There he forged links with Juan Perón – the man who would twice become President of the country, before returning to Italy to found a mattress company and embark on a career as a businessman. Following the military junta in Argentina, Gelli was rumoured to be involved in helping to end Perón's 18-year exile in Spain and return him to Buenos Aires to re-enter the Presidential Palace in 1973. Also in 1973, Gelli rose to the rank of grandmaster of P2.

But in 1974 the GOI proposed that Gelli be banned from Freemasonry and that P2 be expelled from the official list of lodges, and the vote was carried. In 1976 Propaganda Due had its charter officially withdrawn by the Grand Orient of Italy and Gelli was expelled from the Freemasons. P2 didn't disappear, however; Gelli merely took it underground. No longer recognized by the GOI, its very existence was now illegal in Italy – P2 was in direct contravention of Article 18 of the Italian constitution, approved by the Constituent Assembly on 22 December 1947, which stated explicitly that 'secret associations and associations that, even indirectly, pursue political aims by means of organizations of military character, are prohibited'. P2 had become a 'black', or 'covert', lodge, with Gelli becoming known as 'The Grand Puppet Master'. Two of the key members of P2 during its time operating illegally and in the shadows were major figures in Italian banking:

Michele Sindona and none other than Roberto Calvi. Other members were so powerful, and spread across so many key pillars of modern Italian society including politics and the offices of state, that P2 was often referred to as 'a state within a state' or the 'shadow government'. This was, not unlike the Mafia, an organization whose tentacles reached far and wide.

In Peter's mind there seemed to be little doubt that the death of Roberto Calvi was not a murder disguised as a suicide at all – but a very open message. The location where the body was left – Blackfriars Bridge – was no coincidence when you knew that Calvi was a member of P2, Italy's infamous fratelli neri.

The Italian Mafia has had a long and complex relationship with the symbolism and trappings of religion – and of the Catholic Church, in particular. From religious processions stopping outside the houses of Mafia bosses to pay homage to the local godfather, to mafiosi – in fear of arrest if they attend church – bringing their faith home by way of setting up altars and chapels in their houses and hideouts, the iconography of Catholicism was often close at hand. Several major mafiosi were found to have a Bible or prayer book beside their bed, or holy cards on their person, at the moment of their arrest. Some have even quoted passages from the scriptures during their trials.

The metaphysical symbolism present in so much of Catholicism was also widely employed by the Mafia. The fabled initiation ceremony, a blood oath about which I would learn much more as my journey into this world progressed, channelled the Christian idea of fire as rebirth and featured a prayer card prominently in the proceedings. It was a form of baptism, in blood and fire. Similarly, the idea of kissing the hand of the Mafia 'Don' (that honorific itself originating from the Latin *dominus*, meaning lord or master), like kissing the papal ring or the hand of Christ himself, was a sign of respect and submission to a higher power – a power capable of bestowing life or death, of offering protection, food and shelter. Even the word used for those who performed the ultimate act of betrayal and informed on their Mafia brethren – *pentito*, meaning one who is repentant – is steeped in religious inference. And several of those 'penitents' who have turned against the Mafia have claimed their change of heart was due to a religious crisis or epiphany.

The Italian Mafia had since its inception employed the words, actions and imagery of the Church for its own purposes – and operated and communicated using a complex code steeped in religious context. It had also developed its own rules of ritual killing, a grammar of death. Someone who lost face and shamed himself, his family or his clan, was shot in the face. Someone who stole money had his right hand cut off – as this was the hand most likely used to open a wallet. A show of serious disrespect to a senior member might lead to the perpetrator being shot in the legs. For a crime of passion, like cuckolding a Mafia boss, one might be shot in the genitals or castrated. The Cosa Nostra had historically punished traitors using an ancient method that echoes the biblical message of the 'scapegoat' – they had 'goat-tied' the guilty party, tying their wrists, ankles and neck together so that they strangle themselves. The bodies of Mafia victims have often held clues as to why they were killed – eyes, ears, tongues, hands or genitals cut or removed. Items placed in pockets or on the corpse were also steeped in meaning.

And these traditions crossed the Atlantic and were taken up in different forms by the US Mob too. FBI agent Joe Pistone, also known as 'Donnie Brasco', revealed how the Italian-American Mafia would leave a canary on the body of a victim believed to be a snitch or an informant, someone who had 'sung'. When Pistone's own Bonanno family mentor Dominick 'Sonny Black' Napolitano was killed by his own men he had his hands cut off for the sin of introducing an undercover agent to top Mafia bosses – the handshake is the gesture of introductions.

Speaking to Peter it became clear that Roberto Calvi's death wasn't just a murder, it was a symbolic killing designed to send a very specific message. Killing someone as influential as Calvi, and leaving his body to be discovered beneath one of Central London's busiest bridges, was loudly and clearly telling the world that no matter who you are, or where you are, you are never beyond the reach of the Mafia. In Peter's final words to me: 'You can never rest easy, you can never sleep soundly, because wherever you go. . . we'll find you.'

As I left Peter standing beneath Blackfriars Bridge I pondered the fact that, amazingly, the murder of Roberto Calvi is still, more than four decades later, officially unsolved. To try to understand how this could be the case, I travelled to a cosy Italian café a stone's throw from London's historic Smithfield Market to meet someone who could help fill me in. I wanted to know who might have killed

Calvi, and why – and over a strong coffee Professor John Dickie, one of the UK's top experts on the Mafia, laid it out for me. John revealed that at the time of his death Calvi, and his bank, were in deep, deep trouble.

On the morning of 13 November 1977, the citizens of Milan awoke to find banners plastered across the city alleging financial irregularities at Banco Ambrosiano. The claims were anonymous, but they led to a very real investigation into Calvi and his bank. In 1981 Calvi finally stood trial, charged with failing to report $50 million worth of currency dealings to the Bank of Italy, as required by law. He protested his innocence and, awaiting trial, he even tried to kill himself in prison, by cutting his own wrists. Calvi was eventually convicted, and sentenced to prison for four years. Many believe his successful prosecution was only possible because those in power who had up until now been able to secretly protect him, themselves members of the P2, were hobbled by the discovery of an explosive list of the lodge's members during another investigation into rival banker, Michele Sindona.

Calvi lodged an appeal and was set free while awaiting the new trial. Incredibly, he was even able to go back to his job at Banco Ambrosiano and the bank was allowed to trade on the Milan Stock Exchange. This attempt to improve the transparency of the bank instead merely caused it to lose 20 per cent of its value on 5 May 1982, its first day of trading on the exchange. By June 1982, Calvi was running out of time. He had a hearing scheduled for 21 June, at which he was expected to account for the more than $1 billion hole in the bank's finances.

Calvi was getting increasingly desperate in his search for ways to plug the gaps in his finances and keep the bank afloat. On 5 June he signed a typewritten letter to none other than Pope John Paul II, asking for the Vatican's help and requesting an audience with the pontiff so he could explain what had happened. It seems he was ignored. Later, the high-ranking Vatican cardinal Rosario José Castillo Lara would claim that the Pope never received Calvi's letter.

Whatever the truth, now fast running out of options, Calvi took the final, and perhaps fatal, step of getting in touch with Flavio Carboni. It was a decision, once made, that could not be taken back. And it's here that things started to get really dangerous. Carboni was a Sardinian entrepreneur and 'fixer' with ties to criminal organizations in Rome and Sicily, including the infamous Banda Della Magliana, via Giuseppe 'Pippo' Calò, the man known as the Mafia's cashier. It was Carboni, and his underworld connections, who helped Calvi secure a fake passport, his real documents long ago confiscated by the Italian authorities, and flee the country. With his hearing looming, Calvi disappeared.

Calvi was smuggled out of the north-eastern Italian port town of Trieste on a motorboat piloted by Carboni's associate Silvano Vittor. They made their way across the Adriatic to Yugoslavia, and then on to Austria by car. The pair met Carboni in an Austrian town on the Swiss border, and from here Calvi and Vittor headed to Innsbruck, where they boarded a private plane. That plane landed in London on 15 June 1982, less than a week before Calvi's scheduled hearing. By the time he arrived in the UK, Calvi had shaved off his trademark moustache.

Two days later, on 17 June, Banco Ambrosiano voted to remove the now-vanished Calvi as president and dissolve itself. Its shares crashed 30 per cent and its trading on the stock exchange was suspended. That same day Graziella Corrocher, Roberto Calvi's long-term personal secretary, fell to her death from a window of Ambrosiano's Milan headquarters. She reportedly left a note saying: 'May Calvi be double cursed for the damage he has caused the bank and all its employees.' Within 24 hours the body of Roberto Calvi would be found almost 700 miles away, hanging beneath London's Blackfriars Bridge.

I quickly came to realize that Calvi had links to a lot of groups who might want to keep their dealings with him and his bank secret, not least P2, the Vatican and even the Mafia. In fact, in the months before his death, there were even rumours he might have been stealing from his deadliest clients, or that he might have been prepared to come clean on the origins of the money held by his banks in order to save his own skin. What better reason for them to want him dead?

I was curious as to why this Italian banker happened to be in London. One theory suggests he was on his way to America, to join his wife in Washington DC. But the explanation John offers also makes sense – that Calvi was most likely in our capital city, one of the world's global financial centres, in a last-ditch and desperate bid to try to drum up investment to save his bank, and his life. He had contacts in the City, and probably felt London was a safe place, away from the eyes and ears of the Mafia. But John's research painted a very different picture – of a Britain that was home to several dangerous Mafia operatives about whom Calvi may have been unaware. He revealed to me that a man named Francesco Di Carlo had been living in England since the late 1970s. He was a member of the Sicilian Mafia, the Cosa Nostra, and went by the name 'Frankie the Strangler', and I can see how he went on to become a chief suspect for the investigation.

Born in Altofonte, just outside Palermo, on 18 February 1941, Francesco Di Carlo was initiated into the Cosa Nostra in 1966. Elegant and intelligent, he was also an effective drug trafficker, and was made a *capo* (see page vii for a diagram of the structure of the Mafia) in the mid-1970s. But, when a row broke out regarding a drug deal, he was expelled from the Cosa Nostra. It was only due to his valuable years of service to the clan that they did not kill him, but instead sent him into exile. Di Carlo had to leave Italy. He moved to London, and Francesco became Frankie. He became a major drug smuggler and bought a mansion in Woking, Surrey.

Years later, having been arrested and then turned pentito, when he was asked about the hit on Calvi, Frankie explained that yes, he had been approached about the job – by none other than Pippo Calò. But by the time he was able to reply to Calò about it he was told the task had already been given to members of the Neapolitan Mafia, the Camorra. Di Carlo would eventually finger two Neapolitans for the murder. One of them, Vincenzo Casillo, had been assassinated in Rome on 29 January 1983, a bomb igniting under his car when he pressed down the pedal, just six months after the killing of God's Banker. The other, Sergio Vaccari, was silenced even sooner – he was murdered barely three months after Calvi, and in London. A small-time drug dealer, he was not on the authorities' radar, and no immediate links were drawn between him and Calvi. But not only was Vaccari stabbed 15 times, including in the mouth, he was also found with papers relating to P2 on his body, along with several bricks similar to those recovered from Calvi's corpse. It would later be discovered that Vaccari had even been offered the possibility of moving to a new flat by his then-landlord – in Chelsea Cloisters, where Calvi had been living when he was killed.

To my eyes it looked as though not just Calvi but also the man that murdered him – Sergio Vaccari – were killed on British soil. John was quick to agree with me that this seemed the most likely scenario. And yet no one was ever successfully brought to justice for either of these vicious murders committed in England's capital. Having spoken to Peter and now John, I was intrigued. Was the murder of God's Banker a one-off, or were there other active Mafia cells operating in the UK?

I decided to dig a little deeper, but soon found that there are very few newspaper articles from the last 50 years that reference the Mafia in the UK. However, one news report did pique my interest. And it meant taking a train up to the north-west of England, to visit Preston in Lancashire.

Chapter Two

The Lancashire Caravan Park Mafioso

———

As I sat on the train up to Preston I watched the TV news archive one last time. Dating back to 2007, it related the story of the capture of Gennaro Panzuto, an Italian wanted by the authorities in his home country in connection with four murders. He had been on the run for a year, and was finally caught not in Palermo but near Preston. The story seemed far-fetched, and I wasn't sure if this was just a wild goose chase, but I headed north nonetheless.

A caravan park in Lancashire might not seem like the obvious spot to uncover a vital link between the Mafia and the UK, but it was here that I met local resident Mick Bury. He was living in the caravan park when a new neighbour arrived. His name? Gennaro Panzuto. Mick invited me in for a cuppa, and relayed to me the story of how he came to befriend a guy he would only later discover was a Mafia hitman.

Mick told me that his first interaction with his new neighbour was when some local kids knocked on his caravan and told him that 'the Italian guy' had just reversed into his car. Mick went and banged on his door, but was soon placated when the genial young man offered him a generous £200, which would more than cover the damage. The Italian did ask that Mick kept it between them, however – he insisted he must not go talking about it, and he certainly didn't want to get the police involved. As Mick shows me some of his photos of Gennaro it's clear they were friends. The young man in the pictures is handsome, athletic, well dressed. Mick admits Gennaro stood out – he was charming, had some swagger, and was not the typical resident of a northern caravan park. But he was friendly and generous – often buying a round of drinks for his friends and neighbours, and inviting the residents over to his place for barbecues. In Mick's words, 'everybody liked him'.

After just a few months Panzuto left the caravan park. But he didn't go far. He moved to a three-bedroom house on the outskirts of Preston. And he and Mick remained friends. Mick took me to see where this charismatic Italian had lived, and told me that he quite often saw Gennaro entertaining visitors who had flown over from Italy. Mick had no idea about his friend's double life until one day in May 2007, when the house was raided by armed police who demanded to know whether there were any guns on the property. He later learned what had gone on from news reports. He couldn't believe it when he discovered his friend was a Mafia mobster, wanted by Italian police.

I was keen to understand how a man wanted by the Italians for his Mafia associations ended up hiding out in Lancashire, and so

I travelled back to London to meet someone who I hoped could help me to join the dots. Professor Felia Allum is an expert on the Mafia and has tracked this case since the beginning. She explained that the fact that Preston seems such an unlikely home for a Mafia member is its greatest strength. It's the perfect place to hide out, precisely because it is so unlikely. Panzuto was able to become invisible, hiding in plain sight because no one had any reason to look for him in Lancashire.

Felia also highlighted how differences in the respective legal codes in Italy and the UK worked to the Mafia's advantage. In Italy 'Mafia association' is in itself a crime, but in Britain it is not. As a result it seemed more common than I had ever imagined for senior figures from the Italian Mafia to go to ground in Britain.

In 2006 35-year-old Raffaele Caldarelli was arrested at his Hackney shoe shop, which specialized in Italian footwear. He was in fact a senior Camorra boss from Naples, who had lived in London, near his shop, for three years. He was wanted by the Italian authorities for numerous crimes, including Mafia association, extortion and trafficking in drugs and weapons, and in 1995 had been sentenced *in absentia* to 20 years.

In 2012 Gianfranco Techegne was seized in a queue at a post office next to New Scotland Yard in London. He had been on the run for 30 years, and was wanted by the Italian police in relation to the fatal shooting of a policeman during a 1982 jewellery shop raid in Naples. He had seemingly been living for years on the Peabody Estate, not far from London's Metropolitan Police headquarters. Techegne was allegedly a member of the Licciardi crime family, part of the Camorra – the Neapolitan Mafia, based in the city of Naples.

It was clear that for many years Panzuto, and those like him, had found it easier to fall through the cracks, and to evade the authorities, here in the UK – where most of the time no one was looking for them. Felia also confirmed to me that Panzuto was a member of the Camorra and that he was most likely still involved in criminal enterprises while he was hiding out in the UK. Finally, she left me with a lead that I immediately knew I'd have to do my best to follow up – Gennaro Panzuto had been imprisoned in Italy, but had now served his time and left the protection subsequently offered to him in return for the information he had given to the authorities.

I knew that to get the full story I'd have to speak to Panzuto himself. I was determined to utilize all my connections in the UK and Italy to track him down. Before I left her, Felia gave me an in-depth breakdown of the history of the Italian Mafia and its key historical groups. It was to prove invaluable as I navigated their labyrinthine world.

As I'd already learned, the word 'mafia' had originated in Sicily. Here the word *mafiusu* meant swagger, or perhaps boldness or bravado. In the 19th century it was used to imply a man might be an arrogant bully, or equally to suggest he might be enterprising or fearless. The word *mafie*, on the other hand, referred to a local cave system where criminals and fugitives commonly hid out. In the mid-to-late 19th century, as the island navigated the move from feudalism to capitalism and the process of unification (the Kingdom of Sardinia annexed Sicily in 1860, and then became the Kingdom of Italy in 1861), the number of landowners rocketed. And these men needed protection for their land and for their citrus crops and herds of cattle from thieves. With the local police largely ineffective in those days, the citizenry formed their own group for protection – and this was what would eventually evolve into the international criminal organization known as the Cosa Nostra (literally 'Our Thing' or 'Our Cause'), the original Mafia. In the 1950s and onwards the Cosa Nostra expanded into construction and building contracts, and drug and arms smuggling, and became one of the world's most powerful crime groups.

The other famous Mafia group was the Camorra. The Camorra originated in Campania, and in particular in the regions of Naples, Caserta and Salerno. While the Sicilian Mafia grew from the agricultural countryside, the Camorra was much more urban in its essence. Like the Cosa Nostra, the exact origins and 'date of birth' of the Camorra was shrouded in secrecy, blurred by history and the passing of time, and may never truly be pinpointed. However, in 1820 police records document the existence of the Camorra, and the same year the organization's written statute – the *frieno* – was discovered. If it was already a significant and organized group by then, then it's highly likely it dated back to the beginning of the 19th century, if not even earlier. As well as being focused on the city of Naples, another key difference between the Camorra and the Cosa Nostra was its structure. The Camorra was much more horizontal – with numerous families and clans operating as a loose collective. While this did have some drawbacks – the rival groups were often feuding with one another – it had one major advantage over the more pyramidal structure of the Cosa Nostra: it was more resilient, and less likely to suffer as badly if a key senior member was killed or arrested. Like their Sicilian counterparts, in the latter half of the 20th century the Camorra grew in strength and became major drug traffickers, as well as racketeers, counterfeiters and money launderers.

While the Cosa Nostra and the Camorra were far from the only Mafia groups in Italy – and Felia told me of numerous other criminal organizations in the country – they were the two I would keep coming across as I continued my investigation. At least now I had a good grasp of their roots, their similarities and differences, and their place in the history of the Italian Mafia.

As I drove home, my phone started ringing. I pulled over and took the call. One of my network of contacts had come through with a phone number. When I got back home, I immediately followed up the lead – and I was able to confirm that their intel was accurate when I managed to make contact with the man himself. No sooner had Gennaro Panzuto agreed to talk to me than I was on a plane to Italy.

We arrived in Naples and travelled to our hotel to get some rest before filming began the next day. But we were all somewhat surprised when the car pulled up right in the heart of the port itself. And when I say we were staying *in* the port, I'm not exaggerating. That evening, I was in my hotel room getting dressed for dinner when the whole room went dark. But it wasn't a power cut or an eclipse – it was a giant cruise ship passing so close to my window that it blocked out all the light. I could practically see the guests getting ready for dinner out in the town of Naples just as I was. The ship was just metres away, so I carefully drew my curtains before putting on my jacket and heading out to meet the crew.

The next morning, as I was driven through the busy streets of Naples, I prepared to meet a man I was reliably informed had killed several people, unsure of exactly who, or what, to expect. But this was my first chance to speak to someone who had been an active member of the Italian Mafia while living in Britain.

Panzuto had agreed to talk with me on his home turf in Naples. On the way to meet him at an undisclosed location I took the opportunity to drive through the part of town where he grew up – *La Torretta*, the Little Tower. The area in Mergellina took its name from a watchtower built in the mid-16th century by the Duke of Alcalà in a bid to thwart the regular raids from Saracen pirate ships that landed on the beach of the Riviera to kidnap wealthy locals and hold them to ransom. It seemed a fitting spot for a young lad to be indoctrinated into the ways of the local Mafia.

It was here, in among the warren of streets that had once housed the region's fishermen, where Gennaro Panzuto was initiated into the violence of the Neapolitan Camorra. Before I left the UK I had been made aware that Panzuto was not just on the run from the Carabinieri, the Italian police, but also from elements of the Italian Mafia. As I prepared to journey to meet him, he warned me that some of the clans that controlled different sectors of the city still wanted him dead. I was increasingly curious to know what he had done that meant there remained a price on his head.

In order to ensure his safety we had agreed to a strict protocol for our filming. The people that wanted him dead knew he was in Naples, but they didn't know where. To avoid drawing attention to our rendezvous, we arrived extra early to the filming location – and the crew and I all went in separately, one at a time. After our staggered entry we reconvened in a room at the hotel and waited for Panzuto to arrive and to give us the nod that we could go up to meet him. We had to wait quite some time, as Panzuto was understandably cautious and was keen to ensure that no observers would link the arrival of a British television crew hours earlier with his appearance at the hotel. As time ticked by we just had to hope that he hadn't got cold feet, or been spotted. I knew how important this interview could be for my investigation, so when the message finally came that he had arrived safely and was ready to meet with me I think we all breathed a sigh of relief.

When I finally walked through the double doors that took me from the opulent hotel corridor into the spacious suite beyond, the man on the sofa looked up from his mobile phone then stood and walked over. Dressed casually, but not without a hint of Italian style, he was sporting a dark baseball cap, and smiled as he shook me by the hand. This was Mafia captain Gennaro Panzuto. Still fearful for his life, he had insisted on the steps we had taken to ensure the location for our meeting was kept secret, but he proved to be an open and engaging interviewee.

Panzuto began by telling me how he came to be involved with the Camorra. He started off stealing Rolexes, aged just 13 – a brief demonstration on my own wristwatch hinting at the skills acquired in his misspent youth. He confessed his second passion was weapons. As a young man, quick to anger, whenever he clashed with his peers, even over the most trivial of matters, he admitted to me that he would whip out a pistol and – 'pow' – shoot them in the legs. He was soon recruited by a Camorra clan and put to work. Gennaro's new boss had a problem with the boss of a rival Camorra clan. Gennaro was enlisted in the conflict, and sent after the rival's 'soldiers'. He told me that five or six people died in that conflict alone. But this was just the first step on the ladder for Gennaro, as his penchant for violence helped him rapidly ascend the Mafia ranks. His frankness was disarming, his life of bloodshed seemingly a million miles away from the comfortable surroundings of the hotel room in which I found myself.

But, as 2004 arrived, Naples was about to descend into chaos. Two rival Camorra clans went to war over the control of drugs in the city – the ruling Di Lauro clan being challenged by the *Scissionnisti di Secondigliano*. Over 60 people were killed in just 18 months between 2004 and 2005 in what became known as the *Scissionisti* (Secessionist) drug wars, or the Camorra war, one of the bloodiest conflicts in the history of the city. The war was also known as the *faidi di Scampìa* (the Scampia feud), named after one of the key disputed territories in Naples.

The rival group was led by Raffaele Amato, aka *Lo Spagnolo* (The Spaniard). Operating from his new base over the border in Spain, he allied himself with other top Neapolitan mobsters, including Gennaro Marino and Arcangelo Abete. But this aggressive move did not go unnoticed. In October 2004 the Di

Lauro clan responded by killing two of The Spaniard's key men, Fulvio Montanino and Claudio Salerno, gunning them down in a pre-planned ambush. At their funeral, Italian police arrested two Di Lauro hitmen. They were found to be carrying machine guns – it seemed they were there to carry out a massacre. That bloodshed was narrowly avoided, but the killings did not stop. And, as the violence escalated, chaos ensued.

But it was the subsequent murder of 22-year-old Gelsomina Verde by Di Lauro mobsters seeking intel on the whereabouts of another Scissionisti leader that caused widespread outrage and public condemnation. She had until a few weeks prior been in a relationship with the mafioso who had gone to ground, and was tortured before being shot three times in the neck. Her body was then set on fire in her car. In a bid to get a grip on events, and bowing to public pressure, the Interior Minister sent an extra 325 police officers into the city. Soon Naples had more police per person than any city in Europe. Eventually a major police operation on 7 December 2004 led to 52 arrests.

Gennaro went on to tell me that even the army were enlisted in the struggle to maintain law and order – and that for his actions in the war that waged on the streets of his home town he became a wanted man, with numerous people who wanted him dead.

His story was compelling, but I still didn't understand how he went from waging a war in Naples to hosting barbecues on a caravan park in Lancashire. I asked him why he chose to go to the United Kingdom. His answer was disarmingly simple. He had met some British criminals who owned a boat down at the port, and had decided to flee to Britain. When I asked him what he thought of Preston when he first got there his answer – 'For the first time I felt like an ordinary person' – was as surprising as it was honest. But I immediately got it. As I put it to him – 'You're not looking over your shoulder waiting for somebody to come for you with a gun, right?' 'Exactly,' he replied. 'In England my life is normal.'

But Gennaro's 'normal' was not quite the same as it is for the rest of us. He quickly settled back into a life of crime, working on fraud scams with his British criminal contacts. He told me how they maxed out credit cards buying luxury cars. On the run from the Italian police and rival Camorra clans, Gennaro may have been living on a caravan park near Preston but he was soon making money hand over fist. And violence was never far away. Gennaro's role was as a kind of enforcer, he was to ensure that no one got out of control, and if they did step out of line, to put them back in their place in no uncertain terms. I was reminded of his predilection for violence when he explained to me how he did it – by singling out the baddest of the bunch, and biting off his ear. Gennaro knew that the others would be thinking, Okay, if he can bite an ear off, what else can he do? It was violence, intimidation, fear – the hallmarks of the Mafia's method of control, but being utilized with brutal efficiency right here in the UK.

And it wasn't just in the UK that Gennaro was putting his brutality to use. He was also playing a vital role in the ongoing Camorra clan war that was still waging for control of Naples. Despite being in hiding in Preston, he would travel down to Naples by car to murder one of his boss's rivals, and then drive back to

Lancashire. He met my gaze openly when I asked him if he could remember how many lives he had taken. His reply: 'I don't remember the faces, I remember that dull sound – and of course I can still hear it now – when you shoot someone and they drop to the ground.' It was a powerful confession, and I could see the pain, the guilt in his eyes.

What he told me next was a revelation. With the war in Naples spiralling out of control, the bosses of Panzuto's Camorra clan decided they needed to explore every option, including methods to try to end the conflict diplomatically. The senior leadership needed safe territory, away from the scrutiny of the Carabinieri and their rival clans, where they could meet up and thrash out a plan they could put before their enemies. Before he knew it, Gennaro was hosting the entire top brass of his Neapolitan Camorra clan, at his three-bedroom semi in Preston. This summit, to come up with a peace plan, was, if Gennaro was to be believed, one of the gatherings of Italian gentlemen that Mick Bury had witnessed. Gennaro knew that getting the most important men in his clan together in one place for any length of time would be a huge risk in Naples – but in Preston, far from prying eyes and away from the war, the leadership were able to relax and even to chat over a barbecue in the garden. Over two full days they thrashed out a plan to call a truce, all the while hosted by their man in Preston, Gennaro Panzuto.

In September 2005 Paolo Di Lauro was arrested. The Spaniard was already behind bars – arrested by Catalan police after leaving a casino in Barcelona – as were several of the Scissionisti's rival Di Lauro leaders. But during Paolo Di Lauro's court appearance just a few weeks later he famously, and very publicly, kissed one of the Scissionisti leadership – Vincenzo Pariante. Was this a sign that the feud, and the war, was finally over? And had this ostentatious show of forgiveness and unity been brokered over a barbecue in Preston?

Whatever the truth of it, not long after hosting his incredible Preston Camorra summit, the Italian authorities finally managed to track Panzuto down. Arrested in Lancashire, he was extradited back to Italy, tried and convicted of crimes including murder, drug trafficking and Mafia association. He was facing multiple life sentences. After serving 14 years in prison he finally decided to give evidence against the Camorra in exchange for his freedom. He had become a pentito.

For years the Mafia had survived and thrived partially due to their strict internal code of silence and honour, referred to as *omertà*. Loyalty was everything. You did not inform on your fellow members. To be a snitch, a rat, was the very worst thing you could be. This loyalty, and the fear of possible reprisals if you failed to adhere to this code, protected the Mafia for years. In fact, it was not until the 1980s when the first cracks really started to appear, as the Italian authorities went on the offensive against the Camorra in Naples. Only then, during the investigations that would lead to the Maxi Trial that I would later learn much more about, did the first senior Mafia member turn pentito. Until the 1990s it was still an incredibly rare occurrence. And knowing what I did about the Mafia, I understood how huge the decision Gennaro had made in agreeing to give evidence against his former friends in return for his own freedom was.

I asked him if he was not in fear of his life every second of the day. His response surprised me, like so many things about this man and his story: 'I'm not afraid. Why? Today, if you came and killed me, you would do me a favour. You would relieve me from the inner turmoil that I am constantly experiencing. The term [pentito] means a person who regrets what he has done. And today that is what I am.'

After I left the interview with Gennaro I was haunted by his words, and the look in his eyes as he told me this. He was on the brink of tears. This was a convicted killer, a brutal former member of one of the most deadly and violent of all the Italian mafias. And yet he seemed penitent. I'm not sure if you can ever forgive such actions, but I was deeply moved by my time with Gennaro. It was one of the most intense interviews I've ever witnessed.

Having heard his story, and now fully understanding why he had been so keen to keep our meeting secret, we were determined to respect his wishes. If you watch the documentary series you will see that we very deliberately do not reveal the name or location of the hotel. The typical 'establishing shots' that you might expect, showing the front of the building, its name engraved on a brass plaque or writ large above the door, and so forth, are all conspicuous by their absence. It was the least we could do to protect Gennaro from any possible reprisals he might face for having spoken so openly and candidly to me.

Chapter Three

Aberdeen Gets a Taste of Italy

———

Gennaro Panzuto had hidden out – and even arranged a Mafia summit – in Lancashire. He had travelled back to Italy to commit murders as part of the Camorra war in Naples, and had been part of criminal enterprises on British soil. But as I returned to the UK, I began to wonder if Britain might have been more than just a convenient hiding place – that it might even have been home to a full operational Mafia 'cell'.

Back home, I set to work. I combed through page upon page of old news articles in the hunt for evidence of potentially bigger Mafia operations here in the UK. Eventually I came across a story that showed promise, about a restaurant owner in a Scottish city accused of being a Mafia boss. I resolved to follow this lead north of the border – to Aberdeen. One of the UK's northernmost major cities and a full 1,800 miles from Naples, it might seem like an unlikely home for the Mafia – but then again so did Preston.

Until the 1970s Aberdeen was a city built on 18th-century industries: textiles, foundry work, shipbuilding and papermaking, the oldest industry in the city, paper having been first made there in 1694. But by the late 1980s Aberdeen, known as the Granite City, had become a boom town. The reason for its sudden growth? Oil. The first major North Sea oil find had occurred in 1970. By 1975 the infrastructure was built and the oil was flowing from the Forties field, 110 miles east of Aberdeen, all the way to the Grangemouth refinery. As the new offshore oil capital of Europe, thanks to these reserves of the black gold found and tapped beneath the North Sea, Aberdeen was a city on the up. And it was suddenly filled with a new class of cash-rich oil executives used to the finer things in life. With this captive market keen to splash their cash, no eyebrows were raised at the opening of a high-end Italian restaurant in the early 1990s.

I arrived in the city to meet local investigative journalist and crime reporter Norman Silvester. Norman took me to the site of this once-famous local eatery and showed me a photo of the original restaurant. Pavarotti's Italian Restaurant was proudly proclaimed as 'A Real Taste of Italy' on the frontage – and it was 'in more ways than one', as Norman wryly observed. And Norman would know, back in the early 1990s he was investigating criminal activity in the booming Aberdeen. He filled me in on the story.

Pavarotti's was owned by a man named Antonio La Torre who was from Mondragone in Southern Italy. I recognized the name of the town – it's just outside Naples. When I asked Norman about Antonio he told me he was 'very personable, well spoken, very much the ideal host'. But back then Norman's contacts were telling him that there was more to this guy than met the eye. Digging revealed that, back home, the La Torre family were a Mafia clan involved in robbery, extortion, protection rackets, drug dealing and counterfeiting cash. Their criminal activities were generating a huge cash income for the clan, and the family. Norman had caught the scent of a bigger story, and followed his investigator's nose.

Antonio's brother was none other than Camorra crime boss Augusto La Torre, the head of the infamous La Torre clan. Augusto, the younger of the two brothers, had assumed the mantle of leader of the clan from his father Tiberio. Not only was Antonio's little brother involved in importing cocaine into Italy via the Netherlands, he was also later convicted for instigating the 1990 Pescopagano Massacre.

This bloodbath, in which five people died and seven or eight were injured, was part of Augusto's efforts to maintain the La Torre clan's grip on the local drug market. The La Torres were part of the Camorra and were importing narcotics into Italy via the traditional routes from South America. But a new, rival gang of Tanzanians were pioneering what became known as the 'African Connection' – bringing heroin into Italy from Tanzania and Ghana.

On 24 April 1990 gunmen from the La Torre clan opened fire with pistols and machine guns outside a bar in Pescopagano, within their 'home turf' of Mondragone. It was an indiscriminate attack. The first to fall under the hail of bullets were two innocent bystanders, Naj Man Fiugy and Alfonso Romano, neither of whom had criminal backgrounds. Fiugy was an Iranian national, who had come to the bar to play billiards, Romano was an Italian, a house painter who was there innocently drinking a beer. Both died of their wounds.

Haroub Saidi Ally, Ally Khalifan Khanshi and Hamdy Salim were the other three men killed in the shooting. All three were Tanzanians and were believed by the La Torre clan to be drug dealers, and all three were later found to have heroin on them at the time of their deaths. Three Tunisians and a Turk were also injured in the attack. Fourteen-year-old Italian Francesco Bocchetti was in the bar keeping his father, the manager of the establishment, company. He was struck in the spine by a bullet and left paralysed. His father was also injured.

Norman's digging into the family behind Pavarotti's led him to a flat above a butcher's shop in Aberdeen – the home of Antonio La Torre and his family. Antonio had married a Scotswoman in 1982 and the couple had moved to Aberdeen in 1984. It was later discovered that since 1984 Antonio had been wanted by the authorities in Italy for the crime of Mafia association – but his move to the UK, where no such crime existed, helped him keep the Carabinieri at bay. The couple had three children together, and by 1993 Antonio had even become a naturalized British citizen. Norman took me to see the La Torres' family home and it was normal, quiet, discrete – just a regular family home. I was reminded of Gennaro Panzuto's three-bed house in Preston – hiding in plain sight. Like Panzuto, Antonio La Torre seemed to all intents and purposes like a normal family man and local business owner, except for one crucial detail: he was also a member of one of the biggest crime families in Italy.

Following the apparent success of Pavarotti's, La Torre opened a second restaurant in Aberdeen. Norman established that the

Italian was importing products for his burgeoning restaurant business by sea, from Naples straight to the port of Aberdeen. During the same period, Aberdeen was seeing record quantities of cocaine arriving illegally in the city – smuggled by sea. Norman always wondered if the two things were linked – but neither he nor the authorities ever found any evidence specifically linking La Torre to the importation or distribution of cocaine.

Then, in 1996, Antonio was on a 'business trip' in Amsterdam. Given what would later be discovered about the La Torre clan, one might speculate as to what this really entailed – but one thing is for certain: he was finally picked up by the authorities. Extradited back to Italy, the naturalized Brit and charming star of the local Aberdeen restaurant scene was jailed in his home country for Mafia association and firearms offences. However, after 15 months behind bars he successfully appealed and was allowed to return to Scotland. As he had been apprehended in the Netherlands and prosecuted in Italy, it seems his crimes had very little impact on his life back in the UK once he was back in Aberdeen.

But, in 2001, the Italian authorities opened a major new investigation into La Torre's family. Norman told me that they began to tap phones, and picked up numerous calls coming into Italy from Aberdeen. The voice on the tapes was none other than Antonio La Torre. It soon became clear that Antonio was on the phone to his brother in Italy almost every day. They would regularly refer to 'sausages' and 'movements'. But it wasn't really pork they were discussing – it was cash. The wire taps revealed the La Torres were using the restaurants in Aberdeen as fronts to launder up to

£500,000 a month in Camorra cash, turning 'dirty' drugs money into 'clean' currency.

In 2005 Scottish police received an extradition request for Antonio La Torre from the Italian police. But Le Torre got wind of the plan to arrest him, and went on the run. Over several months he traversed Scotland, hiding out in Inverness, Dundee and Stirling. But, running out of places to hide, he ended up back in a flat in Aberdeen – and it was here the authorities finally caught up with him. He had already been found guilty *in absentia* by a court in Naples – sentenced to 13 years for a catalogue of crimes including racketeering, extortion and violence. His extradition was shown on the TV news and, looking back at the archive footage, I can see in the clips of the well-dressed, well-groomed middle-aged Italian man led into the prison transport van in handcuffs a hint of the genial host who must once have welcomed wealthy diners to Pavarotti's. Despite his convictions in Italy, and the fact that he used Aberdeen as his base to run an international criminal enterprise for many years, La Torre was never tried in the UK.

However, this case had merely hardened my conviction that the Mafia were genuinely operating in the UK. This was evidence of a major Camorra crime family washing their money in Scotland, to sit alongside the likely murder of God's Banker by a Mafia hitman in London and the existence of another hardened Mafia killer in Lancashire. And, even though La Torre was the only one arrested in the UK in relation to his criminal activities, I was left in little doubt that he must have had help on our shores. And if he was operating here, there must have been others. For how long had this been going on? I decided I needed to dig deeper, and potentially to go even further back, in order to find the root of Mafia involvement in Britain. And so we began a long, slow journey back down south. A journey that would end in London, and in the capital city's famous East End. . .

Chapter Four

East End Gangsters, Gambling and The Mob

———

Fresh from my trip to Scotland's north-east coast, I was back in England, back in the capital city London, and meeting a man in the East End who I hoped would help me understand just how far back Britain's ties with the Mafia might go. The man who strode confidently down the cobbled street to meet me, his hair slicked back, wearing a tight black turtleneck jumper and dark overcoat, was Stephen Gillen. I was meeting him because, in the 1980s and '90s, he was a major player in London's gangland scene. Now reformed, he had served 12 years in prison for organized crime offences. And, of particular interest to me and my investigation, he had done hard time alongside several member of the Italian Mafia. As we walked the London streets that were once his criminal hunting ground, Stephen told me of his time at Her Majesty's pleasure in the Category A Whitemoor prison, where he met none other than Francesco Di Carlo. It seemed my investigation was coming full circle – Di Carlo, aka Frankie the Strangler, was the man originally suspected of the murder of Roberto Calvi, God's Banker, back in 1982.

As he got to know members of the Mafia behind bars, Stephen gained a rare insight into them – and into the ways their criminal networks functioned. As he told me, 'It's not just an organization, it's a way of life. They are referred into this life, put forward for an initiation process. They would put a picture of a saint in their hand. They would set alight to this, as the saint is burning in their hand they would swear that they would die if they betrayed the codes of La Cosa Nostra.'

In 2007, when Italian police arrested Salvatore Lo Piccolo, the suspected 'boss of bosses' at the time, they found a piece of paper in his house on which was written a list of requirements for anyone wishing to be accepted into the Cosa Nostra. It was dubbed 'The Ten Commandments', and the first entry seemed to perfectly support Stephen's claims. It read: 'I swear to be faithful to Cosa Nostra. If I betray, my flesh should burn.' The actions Stephen described had all the hallmarks of the traditional Italian Mafia initiation ceremony that had its origins in Sicily in the 19th century.

Stephen also laid out for me the regimented hierarchical structure into which the Mafia had evolved: *soldato*, soldier. *Caporegime*, typically shortened to *capo*, the captain – leader of a crew of soldati. Higher up the food chain came the *sottocapo* – the underboss, who was responsible for the capos. Near the top of the pyramid would be the *consigliere* – the adviser – and possibly the *vice-rappresentante*, the vice-representative, who could stand in for the boss in his absence. And at the very top, the boss, aka the don or the godfather. Members of a crew who had not yet become 'made' men, who were not yet fully initiated into the Mafia, were known as 'associates' and were on the bottom rung of the ladder, below the soldati. This template for criminal management was developed over centuries in Italy, but was eventually franchised across the world, adopted by Mafia friends and rivals alike. Strictly hierarchical, this pyramidal structure had clear lines of reporting and responsibility, all designed to ensure the money, power and respect flowed upwards, funnelled to the don. It also kept the individual crews separated from each other and protected both them and their superiors in a way that has subsequently been adopted and refined by modern-day terrorists with their use of 'cells'.

As we walked the streets of London, Stephen and I turned off Hatton Garden, leaving the city's famous diamond district for the part of town known as Little Italy. It was here that, in the 1930s, poor families arriving from rural Italy made their homes in the slums. Stephen told me of the brutal rise of Charles 'Darby' Sabini. As Stephen put it, 'he really comes up the old-school way, which is blood and guts and brutal, street smarts'. And when Stephen said it, I believed it.

Charles 'Darby' Sabini was born on 11 July 1888 to a Scottish woman named Elizabeth Handley. Although the child was given the name Ottavio Handley, his father's identity was uncertain – it seems young Ottavio was the illegitimate son of either Italian immigrant Ottavio Sabini (a carman who drove a horse-drawn cart) or local manual labourer Charles Handley. The boy, who would later become famous as Darby Sabini, grew up in London's Little Italy – at 4 Little Bath Street in Holborn. His mother eventually married Ottavio Sabini on 14 December 1898 and 'Darby' would later take his name and call Ottavio his father. Sabini left school in July 1902, and aged just 13 took up with boxing promoter Dai Sullivan. A promising boxer, the young Sabini was too lazy to train hard, and so became a bouncer. He got a reputation as a hard man following a brawl at the Griffin pub in Saffron Hill – in which he knocked out an enforcer for the Elephant gang (from Elephant and Castle in South London), who had insulted an Italian barmaid. As a result, Sabini became known as the protector of London's Italians – and of the city's women.

We actually filmed a short and surreal sequence with Stephen in the very same Griffin pub that had become Sabini's headquarters. In the end those scenes didn't make it into the final cut of the TV documentary series, but it was one of the stranger filming experiences we had during the shoot. Today the Griffin is what is colloquially termed a 'strip pub'. It's a strip club and gentleman's club. And filming there early on a weekday morning, as the staff got ready for a busy day ahead, was certainly an eye-opener! Unlike some of London's historic boozers, it had changed beyond all recognition since the days of Sabini, so in the end we decided to leave it out of the finished show.

Sabini was soon involved in gambling in the neighbourhood, aligned with influential Jewish and Italian bookmakers. And, as Stephen explained, the protection Sabini offered these bookies was as much from him and his own men as it was from anyone else.

It was a racket, but it was a lucrative and effective one – and Sabini was soon so successful that he had 300 men under him, and even imported gunmen from Sicily. As leader of the Sabinis he was known as the 'king of the racecourse gangs' and the Godfather of Little Italy. He dominated the London underworld, and controlled racecourses throughout the south of England for much of the early 20th century. He rose to become the undisputed Godfather in that era. More recently he has become famous once again, thanks to the portrayal of him in the television drama *Peaky Blinders*. But Sabini wasn't officially a mafioso. He had never sworn an oath to the brotherhood, and his mother was Scottish – to be a member of the Mafia, especially in those days, you really ought to be a full-blooded Italian.

So, given the fact that Sabini wasn't actually Mafia, I asked Stephen when the Mafia itself really came to the UK. His answer? That the Mafia infiltrated Britain in the 1960s. But he was at pains to make a very important distinction: that this was not the Italian Mafia, but the US Mafia, the American 'Mob'.

The Mob was predominantly made up of the descendants of original Sicilian Mafia. They were migrant Italian families who had moved to the United States and then made their fortune selling banned alcohol during the era of Prohibition. First documented in the *New Orleans Times* in 1869, which reported that 'notorious Sicilian murderers, counterfeiters and burglars' had banded together to take over the city's Second District, the first Mafia groups to gain significant influence in the US were in New York – starting in the poor Italian ghettos like East Harlem (known as

'Italian Harlem'), the Lower East Side and Brooklyn before spreading across the city and then across the country, bolstered by waves of immigration from Sicily and Southern Italy in the late 19th and early 20th centuries. The 1890s saw the rise of New York's Five Points Gang. The gang was founded by Paul Kelly – born Franco Antonio Paolo Vaccarelli in New York City but to Italian immigrant parents – who recruited a ragtag collection of local street hoods, many of whom would go on to become some of the biggest names in American organized crime, including Alphonse Gabriel Capone and Charles 'Lucky' Luciano.

Shortly after the end of the First World War, on 16 January 1919, the ratification of the 18th Amendment of the United States Constitution changed America overnight. This was what we now know as Prohibition –when it became illegal to manufacture, transport or sell alcohol. Booze was illegal, but the demand was still there; in fact, if anything it increased. And with this new black market came the potential for huge profit, with bootleg booze prices going through the roof. It was the perfect opportunity for the US Mafia, and they exploited it ruthlessly. The murder rate rocketed, hundreds of thousands of dollars' worth of bonded whiskey was stolen from government warehouses and a tide of alcohol from Canada, the Caribbean and from illegal stills – predominantly in the American Midwest – flooded the country.

This unexpected boom for America's foremost criminal organization coincided with a new influx of Italians, who fled their homeland following Benito Mussolini's rise to power in 1922. One of the biggest groups to relocate stateside? Mafia members –

as Mussolini set about cracking down on his country's organized crime.

In 1931 Lucky Luciano did something that changed the fortunes of the US Mob irrevocably. In a move away from the Italian Mafia's preference for a *capo di tutti capi* (the boss of all bosses) – the idea of having a single boss who ruled them all – he created The Commission. It not only brought all the US Mafia bosses together as a committee, but also ruled over the National Crime Syndicate, which was a loose confederation of American criminal organizations that included not only the Italian American Mafia but also the Jewish Mob and other significant crime groups from across the country. The Commission revolutionized, and modernized, the Mob and organized crime in America.

By 1933 the Mob was so rich, powerful and diversified in its business interests that the end of Prohibition was merely a bump in the road. Money was rolling in from illegal gambling operations, loan sharking, extortion, protection rackets, drug trafficking, fencing and labour racketeering facilitated through the Mob's control of key unions.

The money they made had enabled them to build powerful business and criminal empires. By the 1960s, when Stephen had told me the Mob had begun to involve themselves with the UK, the US Mob – and in fact all organized crime in America – was dominated by New York's 'Five Families'. I was curious as to what tempted the Italian-American gangsters of the 1960s to Britain – and Stephen had a contact who might be able to throw some light on their motivations.

Stephen took me to meet one of his criminal contacts, a man who had encountered the Mob back then. We sat down across the table with Bobby McKew, a 99-year-old reformed gangster and a legend of London's 1960s criminal underworld. Bobby was a dapper gent in a suit and striped tie, a perfectly folded handkerchief poking from his jacket's breast pocket – and whip-smart. It was hard to believe he was just months shy of receiving a telegram from the King, assuming former hardened criminals are also rewarded in such a way for reaching a century not out. His honesty was disarming, as he cheerfully pointed to a photo of London's infamous East End gangsters, the Kray twins, and told me how he liked Ronnie – 'the gay one' – but wasn't so keen on Reggie. He told me that, despite their notoriety, the Krays earned far less than another local crime boss – Billy Hill.

William Charles Hill was born into an established criminal family in St Pancras, London, on 13 December 1911. Aged just 14 he committed his first stabbing. In the late 1920s he took up burglary, and then in the '30s he graduated to carrying out smash-and-grab raids, targeting furriers and jewellers in particular. The Second World War gave him the opportunity to diversify further, and soon he became a major player in London's booming black market, specializing in petrol and foodstuffs. In the 1950s he was suspected of carrying out two high-profile, highly lucrative heists, of a postal van and of a large quantity of bullion. Hill was a mentor of sorts to the Kray brothers. 'Mad' Frankie Fraser served as his bodyguard.

Billy earned a hundred times what the Krays brought in, and Stephen and Bobby agreed that he was the real Godfather of

London at the time. I asked Bobby how he got involved with Billy. He told me how he 'did a few things for him', and he had a glint in his eye when he told me, 'He liked me.'

As the Godfather of London, Billy Hill was uniquely placed to take advantage of a huge opportunity that landed in his lap in 1960 – the legalization of gambling in Britain. Designed to take gambling off the streets and away from criminal ownership, and to do away with the practice of using 'runners' to collect bets, the Betting and Gaming Act was passed by Parliament on 1 September 1960. The act officially came into force on 1 January 1961, and it initially only allowed small sums to be gambled on games of skill such as Bridge. But from May 1961 betting shops were allowed to open. And by 1965 16,000 gambling licences had been granted.

It seemed as if, almost overnight, betting shops and casinos had sprung up everywhere, as Britain swiftly became the biggest gambling nation in the world. I knew that Billy Hill had been in cahoots with club owner John Aspinall, in a con dubbed 'the Big Edge'. In order to ensure the house was always up, a special mangle-like contraption was used to subtly bend the establishment's bespoke cards one way or the other to denote their value. The doctored cards would be re-sealed in cellophane wrapping and delivered back to the club. To all intents and purposes, they appeared to be brand new and unmarked cards. But, with specialist card readers smuggled into the games of chemin de fer – the era's most fashionable card game – on behalf of the Clermont Club, even if the very gentle bends were not always obvious, the tactic ensured that the house was always at an advantage, always had 'the edge'. It was a clever con, and it helped make Billy – and Aspinall himself, who comes across as a rakish, upper-crust con man who rubbed shoulders with Lord Derby, Lord Lucan and Ian Fleming (the author who famously created James Bond) – very rich indeed. His wealth even enabled Aspinall to maintain his very own private zoo. His pride and joy, it featured numerous elephants, gorillas and black rhinos many of whom were born within its confines.

But it seemed Billy Hill might have done more than just fleece punters in casinos – he might have had a share in some of these new venues too. Bobby was told that a single casino could net his boss Billy up to £22 million. And that was the kind of money that, especially in 1960, would make even the American Mafia sit up and take notice.

In fact, just a year earlier global events had conspired to make this new gambling opportunity in the UK even more attractive to the Mob – the Cuban Revolution. In the 1930s Meyer Lansky – a member of the Jewish Mob, a close ally of Lucky Luciano, senior member of The Commission and the man known as 'the Mob's accountant' – had begun to forge ties with Cuba, not only importing sugar and rum but getting involved in the country's casino business. When in 1952 his friend Fulgencio Batista, who had been president from 1940 to 1944, returned to seize power in a military coup, it gave Lansky and his friends on The Commission the perfect opportunity to exploit their relationship with Cuba. The US Mafia invested heavily in Cuban casinos, at one point US Mob bosses owned almost 20.

But then, in 1959, Fidel Castro – having gone to war with the authorities almost immediately after the military coup – finally managed to overthrow Batista's regime. Castro and the Communists had seized control of Cuba – and at a stroke the Mob-controlled casinos in Havana were lost to them. Castro banned all American investment in Cuba. It was a huge blow to the US Mob's financial power. So they must have been licking their lips when just months later gambling was legalized across the Pond. Bobby told me that several Mafia men came over to London – and that they wanted to have a casino. Casinos were not only huge cash cows for the Mob (there's a reason for the saying 'the house always wins'), they were also perfect vehicles for laundering money, thanks to the free flow of cash in and out of such businesses. Bobby explained that Angelo Bruno had visited the casinos of London and that, as one of the big Mob bosses, it would likely have been his money that was to be invested in a UK casino.

Angelo Bruno was born in Villalba, about 100 kilometres from Palermo, in Sicily, in 1910. He emigrated to the US as a child, settling in South Philadelphia. Initially helping out his father in the family's grocery store, he dropped out of school and set up his own grocery business before eventually being accepted into the Philly Mob on the recommendation of convicted murderer Michael Maggio. When he eventually rose to become boss of the Philadelphia family he even spared the life of the man who tried to have him killed, his predecessor as boss Antonio 'Mr Miggs' Pollina. This, along with the fact that he eschewed violence and drug dealing wherever possible, earned him the nickname 'The Gentle Don'.

Bruno was joined in London by fellow mobster Carlo Gambino, the head of the Gambino crime family. Gambino was born into a Sicilian Mafia family in Palermo in 1902. Aged 19, in December 1921 he stowed away on the SS *Vincenzo Florio* bound for Norfolk, Virginia. On his arrival in the United States he immediately headed up the coast to New York City to join his cousins, the Castellanos. He quickly moved up the ranks of the US Mafia, his alliance with Lucky Luciano enabling him to benefit from the internal power struggles that took place and eventually to take control of the Mangano crime family and make it his own. By the 1960s the Gambinos were one of the US Mob's key crime families.

Alongside Bruno and Gambino there was a third mobster, and he was one of the most important men in the whole of the US Mafia – Meyer Lansky, the Mob's money man, the accountant for all the US Mob families and the architect of their hugely profitable expansion into the casinos of Cuba. On Bobby's watch, some of the biggest names from the Five Families were visiting London. These were the architects of organized crime in the United States, and they were scoping out England's capital city with a view to carving out a significant piece of the casino pie.

I was very interested to hear what Bobby told me next: that Billy Hill didn't want the Mob sniffing around his patch. Billy and the other East End gangsters didn't want the US Mafia anywhere near their casinos; they didn't want the Americans muscling in on their business, on their profits. But these were rich, powerful and dangerous men – and, as Bobby put it, 'He wasn't rude to them, I'll tell you that for another thing!'

As part of his efforts to keep his American rivals sweet, Billy had Bobby roll out the red carpet for them. One of Bobby's key responsibilities became taking the Mafia out for dinner. It's moments like these, hearing stories direct from the mouth of a 99-year-old former gangster, that bring these pivotal historical events so vividly to life. I could have spent all day listening to Bobby. But, as he reminded me, all this was really about business, and about money. With Billy and the other London gangsters powerless to stop them, the American Mob quickly took controlling stakes in several London casinos. A key property was the old Colony Sports Club in Mayfair (not to be confused with the present-day Colony Club). The Colony was set up by Meyer Lansky and Angelo Bruno. In the mid-1960s the club even had a Hollywood host and part-owner – George Raft. Raft had worked as a greeter at the Capri Casino in Havana, Cuba. He had even been made part-owner by none other than infamous mobster Santo Trafficante Jr. – the boss of the powerful Trafficante family who controlled much of Florida, was influential in Cuba, was closely allied with Chicago mob boss Sam Giancana, and would later be linked by conspiracy theorists to the assassination of US President John F. Kennedy. Raft had been in Havana the night Castro and his rebels descended on the capital. But in 1966 he was the front man at The Colony – lending his showbiz glamour (this was a man who had appeared in the original 1932 film *Scarface*, as well as *Around the World in 80 Days*, *Some Like It Hot* and *Ocean's 11*) to the Mob's premium London casino, the jewel in their UK gambling crown. Raft's boss, the man running The Colony on the ground, was one of

the men Lansky had entrusted with running his Cuban casinos –
Dino Cellini.

With Bobby and Stephen's help I had pinpointed a key moment
in the beginning of the Mafia's relationship with Britain – the point
at which the US Mob, having lost their Havana gambling operation,
took controlling stakes in the gangster-run casinos of London in
the 1960s.

Before I said my goodbyes to Bobby and Stephen, I asked them
where I should go to truly uncover the breadth and depth of the
Mafia's involvement with Britain. Stephen had no hesitation in
answering: 'America.'

As we parted company, I asked Bobby what he was up to later.
When, with that trademark smile and glint in his eye, he told me he
was off to go partying in Chelsea straight after our interview you
could have knocked me down with a feather. I can only hope that if
I make it to 99 years old, I've got as much gas left in the tank as
Bobby and am partying my way to 100 in style, like he clearly was.

Filled with Bobby's zest for life, and keen to follow up the leads
he had given me, I knew I couldn't afford to hang around in London
any longer. I had a transatlantic flight to pack for. I was off to
America in a bid to find out how deep the US Mob had got its claws
into the UK, and what that meant for Britain's long-term
relationship with the Mafia's particular brand of organized crime.
As they say, if you want to know the truth, follow the money. . .

PART TWO

Chapter Five

The Colony Club

———

An eight-hour flight from London took me to New York City. In the 1960s, when the US-based Mafia were muscling in on the burgeoning London casino scene, the Big Apple was the power base for the Five Families: Gambino, Bonanno, Colombo, Genovese and Lucchese. These were the Sicilian immigrant crime syndicates who built empires in the land of opportunity and formed the American Mob. Racketeering, politics, construction, the unions – over the course of the 20th century almost no part of American life was left untouched.

In the late 19th century, there had been a wave of Italian immigration into America and in particular into the New York area. The turn of the century saw the rise of the Five Points Gang under Paul Kelly and the emergence of the likes of Al Capone and Charles 'Lucky' Luciano. During the Prohibition era, in the 1920s, New York's criminal underworld distilled into two main factions – the group led by Giuseppe 'Joe the Boss' Masseria, that would later become the Genovese crime family, and that led by Salvatore 'Little Caesar' Maranzano. In 1930, the two rivals went to war.

What became known as the Castellammarese War raged for over a year until, on 15 April 1931, Masseria was murdered at a restaurant on Coney Island, thanks to the collusion of one of his men – Lucky Luciano. It was believed Masseria was shot from behind, a hail of bullets striking him in the head, back and chest, while he was sitting playing cards at the restaurant. Victorious, Maranzano divided up New York – and created the original Five Families. But he made himself the capo di tutti capi, the boss of all bosses, and within six months he had been killed on the orders of his own man, the turncoat Lucky Luciano. Lucky had been alerted to a plot by Maranzano to have him killed – and decided to strike first. He sent four Jewish mobsters, their faces unknown to his boss, sourced with the help of Meyer Lansky and his associates, to Maranzano's office. Here, disguised as government agents, they disarmed his bodyguards and stabbed the boss multiple times before finally shooting him dead. It was then, as I had previously learned, that Luciano established The Commission, doing away with the position of the capo di tutti capi for good and creating a flat structure at the top of the Mafia organization with each of the main families getting an equal say and a seat at the table.

I collected my hire car and drove the short distance from John F. Kennedy International Airport to Ozone Park, in Queens. This was part of the Gambino family's turf, and I was about to meet a man who had worked for both the Colombo and the Gambino crime families in 1970s New York. That man, waiting for me on the pavement outside some nondescript shuttered business premises, all white-toothed grin and cream cashmere rollneck, was the former Mafia associate Salvatore 'Crazy Sal' Polisi. Like many of the hardened criminals, gang members and organized crime contacts I'd met, not just in this investigation but across my career, he was disarmingly jovial. And he seemed thrilled I'd travelled so far to see him, and to hear his tales of the old days. For my part, I was excited to be hearing about the Gambino and Colombo families, and their relationship with gangsters and casinos back in Britain, from a man who had grown up working for them on these mean streets.

Sal told me that he had a reputation for a temper, and for violence – not unlike Gennaro Panzuto, it struck me. In fact, he had erupted on someone in the very building outside which we were standing. One night a big guy, 6'3", 240lbs, who had killed 'a bunch of people', was being abusive. Sal had heard enough. He stepped in and, in his words, 'took him apart'. I could only imagine what that must have looked like. Their fight spilled out into the street, where Sal smashed the other man's head, pulled off his ear and beat him so badly he had the guy's teeth embedded in his knuckles.

I'd also heard tell of how he had once tied a guy to a pool table and sliced underneath the back of his testicles, before punching him in the face – breaking his nose and leaving him tied there. All for sleeping with a mob boss's girl. In his heyday, Sal had two girlfriends and 'a wife back at home raising babies'. He owned 11 sports cars, wore flashy Rolex watches – and once spent a million dollars on a racetrack. He loved to hit the clubs, and even opened his own – the Sinatra Club in Queens, which became an infamous hangout for his fellow mafiosi. One of the regulars was Henry

Hill – the mobster who would turn informant, and whose story was famously told in the Martin Scorsese film *Goodfellas* in which he was played by Ray Liotta. Although he has admitted to plenty of violence and criminality, and once had a whole cache of weapons including hand grenades and guns – Sal has always denied ever killing anyone. But make no mistake, this guy had been a serious mobster back when the US Mafia were in their pomp.

As we walked through the old neighbourhood, Sal gave me a Gambino family history lesson. By the mid-1970s the Gambino family was run by the infamous Mafia don Paul Castellano. It was an era when the Mob, at the height of its power, felt it could operate with impunity. Sal had no qualms about pulling off a $2 million gold robbery – and this was back in 1973, when gold was $60 an ounce. That's over 15,000 kilograms of gold he had hauled off. But for Sal it was normal – and the risks were low, as back then there were no CCTV and security cameras, no standardized DNA testing, no significant network of police informants. It was so easy that, in his own words, Sal and his fellow mobsters felt they had 'a licence to steal'.

Our stroll through the neighbourhood of Ozone Park had brought us to a restaurant and bar called Gt Kingston – but Sal explained to me that back in the day this place was called Robert's Lounge, and then the South Side Lounge. From the outside, to the untrained eye, it was just like any other drinking establishment. But back then the basement of the bar was where all the action was – it was a Mafia-run gambling joint and one of Sal's regular hangouts. It also seems to have been a graveyard for anyone who crossed the Mob – in 1980 a human leg bone and a portion of a human shoulder bone were excavated from the South Side Lounge basement. News reports at the time suggested they were the remains of Thomas 'Tommy Two Guns' DeSimone and Martin Krugman. The pair were known associates of James 'Jimmy the Gent' Burke – who was rumoured to have been the mastermind of the 11 December 1978 Lufthansa Airlines robbery, a $5.8 million heist perpetrated at John F. Kennedy International Airport and the biggest cash theft in US history. Jimmy the Gent was believed to have links to the man who ran his criminal operation from the bar's basement – Paul Vario, a senior member of the Lucchese crime family. This was a location steeped in criminal history.

We sat down in a basement booth, and Sal told me his family story. His father had driven a horse and wagon in New York in 1929, in the era of Prohibition. He would drive his wagon out to the eastern part of Long Island where ships arrived carrying cases and cases of whiskey. Many of those vessels originated from the UK. Sal's dad would load up the illicit booze and drive it back to Brooklyn, where it could be distributed. Sal's own family had already given me a direct link between America's Italian-American Mob and the UK – way back in the late 1920s and early '30s. It wasn't just booze from Canada, the Caribbean and a network of illegal Midwest stills that the Mob had access to – Britain's supply of contraband alcohol during Prohibition had also been a big part of helping to build the Mafia in America.

But there was another more recent link, the story that had brought me out to the US in the first place, that I was keen to see if my new friend could help shed light on. What could Crazy Sal Polisi tell me about London's casino scene, East End gangsters and the US Mob?

Sal informed me that he had been in the Lewisburg Federal Penitentiary in 1975. Here he got to know two 'made' members of the Philadelphia Mob, which back then was run by the Gentle Don, Angelo Bruno. Sal occasionally heard these Philly mobsters talk in prison about a casino operation based in the UK, known as 'The Colony Sports Club' – a casino business that Angelo Bruno had 'a piece of'. It was this new lead, confirmation from Sal's eight-year stint inside, that Angelo Bruno had a share in London's old Colony Sports Club casino, as I'd originally been told by Stephen Gillen and Bobby McKew, that sent me to my next destination stateside: Philadelphia.

We hopped back into the hire car and headed out of town on the New Jersey Turnpike. This road out of the Big Apple is the same one filmed for the famous title sequence of *The Sopranos*, the TV drama series that is perhaps the single most comprehensive study of the inner workings of an (admittedly fictional) Italian-American Mafia family. As we drove the turnpike, New York slowly giving way to New Jersey, the stop signs and traffic lights, the storefronts and city parks whizzing past the window, I really did feel like I was journeying into that world, the world of Tony Soprano, the world of the US Mob.

And so we drove just shy of 100 miles south of New York, to one of America's most dangerous cities: Philadelphia. Someone had told me that it was one of the most dangerous places on earth, that it had a higher murder rate even than Cali in Colombia – whether or not that was true, it was certainly the location that our health and safety advisers back in the UK were most concerned about so far. As a result, we stuck to a very rigid plan. First up we headed straight to Little Italy. When we arrived it was lunchtime, so I took the opportunity to sample the local delicacy – the infamous Philly Cheesesteak. It didn't disappoint. Thinly sliced grilled beef steak, melted cheese, onions, peppers and pickle – all on a long roll the Americans call a 'hoagie'. Just the thing after a morning filming and a hundred-mile drive. We did some filming of the neighbourhood, and even managed to get the drone up to capture some aerial shots, but soon it was time to call it a day.

The next morning, we headed out bright and early onto the streets of Philadelphia. I was in town to meet former Philly Mob member George 'Cowboy' Martorano. George, his silver hair combed back, eyes hidden behind dark glasses, met me on a street corner – and told me he was raised on Gunman's Row, where guns for hire would hang out waiting for business, and those in need of an assassin would drop by to hire them to kill someone for them for cash. He told me that the main Mafia faction in the city, the Philly family, had joined forces with the Five Families in the 1950s. The territory belonging to George's Godfather, Angelo Bruno, head of the Philly family, was the biggest of all the Mob bosses – stretching from Newark, New Jersey, through Philadelphia, and all the way to Baltimore. A shrewd businessman, the Gentle Don was also the man who controlled the gambling business in three states. It was a huge part of his operation. It was big business, and Bruno loved it.

George confirmed that Bruno had heard about what was happening in London with the casinos, and went for it – making a deal that soon saw money travelling back and forth across the Atlantic.

I had already heard that Bruno was involved with London casinos, but no one had ever documented how the American side of this transatlantic partnership worked. I was finally talking to a man who might be able to tell me more about this seminal moment in Britain's relationship with the Mafia. And George did not disappoint. He told me how he and his Mob peers would arrange junkets in London – chartering planes to fly US high-rolling gamblers to London as guests of the club and hosting them for up to a week at a time. George and his colleagues would offer big-money gamblers the chance to go and bet in London – but they had to be prepared to put up a $200,000 stake. The offer was nevertheless so appealing that George managed to fill two planes a month with gamblers from Philly, South Jersey and New York. And the Philly family were getting paid twice – not just the junket fees charged to these 'whales' but also their cut of the losses they would rack up in the London casinos in which Angelo Bruno had a share. It was win-win for the Mob. However, there was one major catch: the Mob's undeclared profits from the casinos in London were on the wrong side of the Atlantic. So how did the Americans get their money?

George's family were part of a solution that was brilliant in its simplicity. George's father went over to London with his wife, George's mother. They had had a fur coat specially tailored for her – it had a zipper on the inside, and an array of pouches hidden in the lining. George estimated that each pocket might have been able to hold between ten and twenty thousand US dollars, meaning that when they flew back to the US his mum was probably wearing a coat weighing more than she did – and stuffed with upwards of $300,000 in cold, hard and now completely untraceable cash. That $300,000 in 1965 would be worth nearly $3 million in 2024.

I could tell that this kind of money was unlikely to have been allowed to be siphoned off and sent abroad without the knowledge and permission of local London gangsters. I asked George if he knew who Angelo Bruno was directly doing his UK business with. His unflinching answer was Ronnie and Reggie. So it was the Kray twins who were the Philly Mob's London partners, and the conduit for significant US Mafia involvement in Britain.

On 24 October 1933 Reginald Kray was born in Haggerston, East London. Just ten minutes later his mother Violet gave birth to his twin brother, Ronald. Reggie and Ronnie were identical twins. Their dad was a travelling rag and bone man with a penchant for booze, and then later a deserter – he was conscripted during the Second World War, then fled and lived on the run in the UK for 15 years. As a result, the boys were raised entirely by their mother. They took up amateur boxing, Ronnie in particular showing signs of the aggression and violence that would become the brothers' trademark. It has been speculated that one reason for Ronnie's simmering rage was his need to repress his sexuality.

Having absconded from their National Service, and then gone absent without leave (AWOL) from the army, and assaulting a police constable, they were arrested and were among the last inmates to be imprisoned in the famous Tower of London. As they were moved around various military prisons their behaviour worsened. Eventually they escaped, but were captured and prosecuted as civilians, sentenced for the crimes they had committed while AWOL.

Their criminal records put a stop to their boxing careers, and the Kray twins turned to crime full time, predominantly running protection rackets and indulging in armed robbery, hijacking and arson. They named the criminal organization they built 'The Firm' and modelled it on the gangs of the Chicago underworld in the 1920s made famous by Al Capone. Their big break came when they were able to purchase a nightclub, Esmerelda's Barn, in London's glitzy West End. Suddenly these dapper, but dangerous and somewhat dim, twins were local celebrities. They rose to prominence in the Swinging Sixties, and were photographed by David Bailey and hung out with the likes of Frank Sinatra, Joan Collins, Sammy Davis Jr., Diana Dors, Judy Garland, Barbara Windsor, Liza Minnelli, Cliff Richard, Dusty Springfield, Shirley Bassey and even former Hollywood star turned Colony Club 'host with the most' George Raft. The twins loved George in particular – for his role in their favourite gangster flick, the original 1932 *Scarface* directed by Howard Hawks and produced by Howard Hughes. Ronnie and Reggie were the acceptable face of organized crime, popular anti-establishment figures who pioneered a form of British 'gangster chic'.

George remembered the Krays as gentlemen, partners who gave them no problems – and told me the Americans only found out quite how crazy these East End gangsters were many years later. When Bruno and the Philadelphia Mob were partners in the likes of the old Colony Sports Club, Ronnie and Reggie were running protection rackets at the main London casinos. And George had an incredible story to tell me about them, a story that had never been heard before.

In the mid-1960s George's Godfather, Philly family boss Angelo Bruno, had invited Ronnie Kray over to Philadelphia. Ronnie being Ronnie, he had travelled with a large quantity of cash. He flew into LaGuardia Airport in New York – but on his journey to Philadelphia was tailed by Philly city police who had been alerted to his presence and were investigating gambling in the city. They waited until Ronnie was safely in their jurisdiction, sitting down for a meal with Angelo Bruno at a local restaurant, before entering and arresting both Ronnie and Angelo – and grabbing Ronnie's suitcase full of cash. The unlikely pair were taken to the detective's division on 22nd and Jackson. A trial for the city's Mafia godfather alongside one of London's biggest gangsters would have been a disaster for the Mob. Fortunately the pair made bail, but Ronnie was on a short tourist visa and the clock was ticking. The Mob knew they needed to stop this going to trial, not least because the judge assigned to the case was one they knew they might struggle to influence.

The Philly Mob went into overdrive to use their reach to influence the legal proceedings. George's dad was the man entrusted with ensuring this embarrassing and potentially hugely damaging problem went away. George himself was even with his father, at City Hall, as he pressed to get the arraignment hearing held as quickly as possible and then – using a court runner who the Mob had control over to pass on the message – to get the case thrown out by the presiding judge. It was a classic Mob move – to infiltrate organizations and pillars of state and leverage the little guy in order to influence the true power broker, the big decision maker. And it worked. Whatever the detail or true nature of the communications between the runner and the judge, the case was dropped. They'd done it. Angelo Bruno and Ronnie Kray would not be going to trial. With the case dropped, Ronnie was free to leave the country, which he promptly did. Not only that, with the charges removed he even had his suitcase of cash returned to him. It was an incredible story, a true first-hand account of a lost chapter of the history of the Krays, the Mob and the links between the Mafia and Britain.

Then, off camera, as George and I continued to talk about Ronnie's visit to Philadelphia, he alluded to a visit the younger of the Kray twins might have made to Las Vegas. It was unclear from what George told me whether this might actually have taken place immediately after the incident he had just related, perhaps before Ronnie returned to the UK, or whether it had occurred on a completely separate occasion, on another trip to America. Either way, it sounded intriguing, and a possible new link between the Mafia and Britain. I was determined to dig more into it.

Chapter Six

Englishmen and The Mob

One thing I hadn't heard much if anything about so far was whether any Brits had ever been part of the US Mob. I knew British gangsters had worked hand in glove with their transatlantic criminal cousins, but had anyone ever crossed the Pond and been accepted into the American Mafia? When I got some spare time, I took the opportunity to do a little research – and I came up with two key names, and two fascinating stories.

The first was Owen Vincent Madden. 'Owney' was born in Leeds in 1891. His parents, Frances and Mary, were Irish immigrants. Owney's dad died not long after he was born, and the widowed Mary placed him and his sister Mary and brother Martin in an orphanage before sailing for New York and a job as a scrub maid. By the time Owney was four years old his mother had saved up enough from her wages to pay for tickets for her three children to join her in America. But on the streets of Hell's Kitchen the young Owney grew up quick, and he grew up mean. He learned to fight, and to use weapons including slingshots, blackjacks, knuckledusters, brickbats, lead pipes and stilettoes – long, slender, needle-like daggers. Aged just

14 he carried out his first major violent crime, badly beating a man in the street and stealing $500 from him. He grew to have a penchant for using a lead pipe as his weapon of choice. By the age of 21 he had become the leader of a fearsome local Irish street gang known as the Gopher Gang – and he'd upgraded his arsenal: he now packed a Smith & Wesson revolver.

In September 1911 he shot and killed a member of the rival Hudson Dusters gang – bohemians with a penchant for cocaine – deep in the heart of the Dusters' territory. His reputation was such that he stood over this dying victim and brazenly shouted out, 'I'm Owney Madden, 10th Avenue' – and yet no witnesses came forward, and he was never charged with the murder. Less than five months later, in February 1912, he clambered aboard a busy New York streetcar to remonstrate with a store clerk with whom he had got into a heated argument over a woman. He shot the man in the face. As he lay dying, the clerk named Madden as his murderer. But, having intimidated and even 'disappeared' eyewitnesses in both cases, Owney was never brought to trial for either of the two murders. Owney was the most feared man in the area, and given the nickname 'The Killer'.

But nine months later the Dusters got their revenge. Owney had turned up to a dancehall that was outside the Gophers' territory. He was surrounded by Dusters and shot 11 times. In the local Flower Hospital, Owney's doctors removed six bullets from his body, but Owney refused to name his assailants. The physicians were unable to extract the remaining five slugs, however, and these would remain lodged deep in his body for the rest of his life.

While he was recovering, Owney's leadership of the Gopher Gang came under threat from his love rival and fellow gangster William 'Little Patsy Doyle' Moore. After several years of attacks on his men and his operation from Moore, Owney had had enough. He used the woman he had stolen from Moore, Freda Horner, to lure his nemesis to a bar where his men shot him. Moore managed to stagger out of the establishment, but died on the steps outside. This time Owney was arrested and tried – and in June 1915 a jury found him guilty of first-degree manslaughter for ordering the hit on Moore. Owney was sentenced to 10 to 20 years in Sing Sing prison.

Owney was released after eight years, his sentence cut short for – incredibly enough – good behaviour. But the world he re-emerged into had changed beyond all recognition. America had fought in the Great War, jazz had exploded into the mainstream, and the era of Prohibition had begun. The Gopher Gang had fallen apart, but bootlegging ushered in a whole new world of criminal opportunity as the Roaring Twenties took flight. Soon Owney was at the head of one of the biggest bootleg syndicates in America, alongside fellow local gangsters Bill Dwyer and Frank Costello. 'Big Bill' Dwyer was an Irish-American, but Costello (born Castiglia) was Italian-American – and a close friend of Charles 'Lucky' Luciano, and would go on to become the boss of the Luciano crime family. I had also heard about how Costello was close with Joseph Kennedy – the father of future president John and future attorney general Bobby. There has been a lot written about how Joe used his Mob connections, especially a major player in Chicago called Sam Giancana, to help his son defeat Richard Nixon in the battle for the

White House – but how Bobby's crusade against organized crime might have ultimately turned the Mob against him and got both him and his brother, 'JFK', killed. It's one of modern history's most fascinating and enduring conspiracy theories – but I had to force myself not to go down that rabbit hole.

Back in the era of Prohibition, the fearsome trio of Madden, Dwyer and Costello ran 'The Combine' together – a huge rum-running operation based in New York. Owney invested in the city's speakeasies and bars – giving him some control over, and profit from, the outlets for his illegal booze. He bought the Club Deluxe from former heavyweight boxing champion Jack Johnson, turning it into the Cotton Club. He cosied up to corrupt politicians, invested in theatres and nightclubs – his venues drawing crowds to see performers including Louis Armstrong and Duke Ellington. And he began to systematically take over the growing and only recently legalized sport of boxing. He even had a cut of Max Baer – who would eventually become the heavyweight champion of the world, and famously defeated Adolf Hitler's favourite boxer, the German former world champion Max Schmeling in an epic fight at Yankee Stadium. Owney was driven through Manhattan in his luxury, Indiana-made bulletproof Duesenberg car accompanied by blonde bombshell and darling of Broadway Mae West, or chronicler of the city, author and journalist Damon Runyon. His chauffeur? A young lad with dreams of making it big in Hollywood named George Raft. 'The Killer' had transformed into 'The Duke of the West Side'.

But his time in New York was ended by a swift one–two in 1933. First came the end of Prohibition, which pulled the rug out from under his bootlegging empire. And then the attentions of a new district attorney saw Owney spend a year back in Sing Sing for a parole violation. Enough was enough, and Owney got out while the going was still good. He found himself a new town with just the right level of lawlessness for him to thrive – Hot Springs, Arkansas. Here he invested in local spas – and in The Southern Club casino, where he held prize fights, and played host to his many famous friends and clients including Max Baer and Rocky Marciano.

In 1936 Lucky Luciano fled New York and sought refuge in Hot Springs. When he was arrested, his old friend from the Big Apple, Owney Madden, tried to bribe the Arkansas attorney general with a $50,000 offer in return for helping Lucky fight extradition back to New York. The attempt backfired, and two months later Luciano was convicted of compulsory prostitution and sentenced to 30 to 50 years in state prison. It was then that he eventually made Frank Costello the boss of what was now the Luciano crime family.

Incredibly, Owney stayed out of jail and lived to the age of 73. He died of natural causes – a miracle given the events of his youth – in his adopted home of Hot Springs in 1965.

Owney's was a fascinating tale of a boy who went from an orphanage in Yorkshire to being one of the most infamous and wealthy criminals in New York during Prohibition. But even though he had strong links with the likes of Lucky Luciano, Frank Costello and even Mob money man Meyer Lansky, he wasn't truly a member of the US Mob. Yet as I dug a little deeper I thought I might just have found a Brit who had that dubious honour, and he wasn't who I had expected at all. . .

Wilf Pine was born on 23 February 1944 in Newcastle. At the age of 15, having rebelled against his violent father and turned to petty crime, he was sent to the Wellesley Nautical School – a 'last chance' school, at an old First World War submarine base at Blyth, Northumberland, where troublesome teenagers were sent by the courts to try to finally instil some discipline in them through seafaring. Here, over the course of two years, he learned to fight, and began making friends with boys who would later become violent and powerful men and who already had connections with the UK's criminal underworld.

When he left Wellesley, Wilf began running a team of bouncers who manned the doors of the clubs on the Isle of Wight, to where his mother had moved. Thanks to his criminal connections, and the growing overlap between the vibrant music scene of the island and London's gangsters during the Swinging Sixties, Wilf got to know East End hard men Ronnie and Reggie Kray. He clearly impressed the twins. Famous fellow London gangster Charlie Richardson has quoted Reggie Kray as saying Wilf was 'the most fearsome fighter I've ever seen. He was lethal. He was a fucking animal.'

Wilf eventually became Ronnie Kray's business manager and best friend – and the Kray twins bankrolled his setting up of his own music production business. Soon Wilf was managing bands of his own, and the Krays were exploring the idea of expanding into the music business – it's rumoured they even attempted to prise The Beatles away from Brian Epstein before settling for blackmailing him over his secret homosexuality.

In no time Wilf was working for legendary music manager Don Arden, who was Sharon Osbourne's dad and looked after Black Sabbath among many others, including the Small Faces. The imposing Wilf was put to work by Don – known as the 'Al Capone of Pop', 'Mr Big' and the 'English Godfather' – as a minder for famous Birmingham supergroup The Move. Soon after he became the co-manager of Black Sabbath after they visited Don Arden's offices. But he didn't leave his gangsterism behind. The band's co-founder and guitarist Tony Iommi remembers Wilf carrying around a big case containing a hammer – to 'kneecap' anyone who didn't pay the band their dues. Wilf would later manage Stray, before the band were taken over by none other than Ronnie and Reggie's older brother Charlie Kray.

But the true depth of Wilf's incredible story only came to light when he met Kray biographer John Pearson at Charlie Kray's funeral. Pearson was struck by the fact that in the church in Bethnal Green the greatest gangsters of the 1960s and '70s, including Charlie Richardson, 'Mad' Frankie Fraser and Freddie Foreman, were all showing a man he did not recognize a significant amount of respect. Pearson would only later discover that this was Wilf Pine, a man so feared and respected that his name had flown under the radar and had barely appeared in any accounts of the UK's gangsters and criminal underworld of the '60s and '70s. But known as 'The Englishman', he was perhaps even more famous, and even more feared, in New York than he was in Britain. This was all because he had become the adopted son of Joseph Luco Pagano, a senior member of the Genovese crime family – one of the original Five Families of the New York Mob.

In the late 1960s and early 1970s Wilf was travelling regularly to the United States on music business. It was on these visits that he met and got to know Joe Pagano, and the Italian-American mobster took the Brit under his wing. Joe was a literal and metaphorical father to Wilf, adopting him as his own and taking the place of the violent dad Wilf wished he'd never had. He was even best man at Wilf's wedding. And he introduced his surrogate son into the inner workings of the US Mob.

It seemed Wilf Pine was the first Englishman ever to be invited to be part of the US Mafia. He was an 'associate' in the Genovese family and a trusted friend of Joe Pagano. He was family. In the early 1970s Wilf Pine led a double life, continuing his work in the music business while becoming increasingly involved with many of the most powerful figures in organized crime in America, including the flamboyant John Gotti and the Genovese's powerful 'front boss' from 1972 to 1981, Frank Alphonse 'Funzi' Tieri.

I even found a photo online purporting to be of Wilf posing with Genovese wise guy Robert Milano, caporegime Daniel Pagano, soldato Charles 'Fat Charlie' Salzano and Joey Cusumano – a key man in the Chicago Mob's Las Vegas operation.

I'd never heard of Wilf Pine, but it seemed he was a man who'd had more connections with British gangsters and American mobsters than almost anyone else. Sadly for my investigation, I learned he had died in 2018 and I'd missed my chance to meet the quiet legend that was Wilf Pine.

Chapter Seven

A Sin City Segue

———

I had done a little digging into Mafia and Mob connections to Las Vegas before I began my investigation in earnest, as had the production team, but we failed to come up with any major leads. And, given the time and cost associated with adding an entire West Coast leg to my trip, we'd decided against it. But now, reading about Joey Cusumano, the Chicago Mob, Las Vegas, and about the links between Wilf and the Krays, I suddenly remembered George Martorano's off-the-cuff remark about Ronnie Kray and Vegas. Redoubling my efforts, I eventually dug up a fascinating new story – one that appeared like it might corroborate George's comment.

It seemed that in the late 1960s – around the time I'd been told by George that Ronnie had been arrested in Philly with Angelo Bruno – he had indeed also visited the town known as Sin City: Las Vegas, Nevada. This was according to a man named James Campbell, who had got to know the Krays in the 1980s, had gained their trust, and had worked as their publicist. He had helped the twins to negotiate book deals while they were behind bars in Britain.

I knew about the East Coast US Mob's interest in casinos in both Cuba in the 1950s and London in the early 1960s. But the evolution of gambling in Las Vegas, 2,500 miles west of the power base of the Five Families in New York, was a much older story.

Las Vegas was founded in 1905 as a settlement in the basin of the Mojave Desert in Clark County, and incorporated (meaning it had elected officials and was recognized by state law) in 1911. Crucially for the fledgling city, it was able to weather the worst effects of the Great Depression – which decimated American life between 1929 and 1939 – thanks to two key events that took place in 1931. First, the state of Nevada voted to legalize gambling in a bid to kickstart the local economy. And secondly, construction began on the Hoover Dam – a massive hydro-electric project on the Colorado River just south-east of Las Vegas. Both events brought workers to Vegas and helped grow the population and the economy. The creation of a major military base near by in 1941, originally the Las Vegas Army Airfield but renamed the Nellis Air Force Base in 1950, helped continue the city's upwards trajectory during the Second World War and in the years after. In those post-war years the expansion of the hotel and casino industry turned Las Vegas into the gambling capital of the world.

Eventually the focus of many of the new developments would move from Downtown to 'The Strip' – a part of Vegas that is actually outside the official city limits, where the huge new hotels, casinos and entertainment venues that have become synonymous with Sin City are built on unincorporated land. The majority of this development in the 1940s and '50s was driven by individuals associated with the US Mob. Vegas was regarded as an 'open city', which meant any Mafia group was free to invest there. No one family owned or controlled the town, the hotels and casinos or the gambling there. But that didn't mean it wasn't Mob-run. A prime example is The Flamingo.

In 1945 William Richard 'Billy' Wilkerson, a real estate developer and the founder of the *Hollywood Reporter*, bought a large plot of land in Paradise, Nevada, along US Route 91 – in the area that would become famous as 'The Strip'. Short of funds for his ambitious hotel and casino project, he partnered up with a trio of mobsters – principal among them Benjamin 'Bugsy' Siegel. Bugsy was a key member of one of the US Mob groups I had focused somewhat less on – the Jewish Mob. But he and his close friend Meyer Lansky, both members of this branch of the wider American Mafia, were important figures in the story of organized crime in the States and the rise of the Mob. Both were vital parts of the National Crime Syndicate.

Bugsy pushed out Wilkerson and, with tacit support from Lansky, took on the Flamingo project alone. But under his watch costs spiralled from $1 million to $6 million. Nevertheless, on Boxing Day 1946 the casino did finally open – and one of the special guests was none other than Hollywood star and friend of the Mob, George Raft – the man who would later help front the US Mafia's foray into gambling in the UK at the Colony Sports Club. But stormy weather and faulty air conditioning made the grand opening a damp squib, and it was reported as such by the press. To make matters worse, a lack of available finished suites to tempt guests to stay meant gamblers at The Flamingo were staying at two rival hotels near by – El Rancho Vegas and Hotel Last Frontier. Soon the casino was struggling to overcome its bad reputation and the gaming tables were losing money. By late January 1947 it was temporarily closed.

The Flamingo reopened on 1 March 1947 as a casino but now with a fully operational three-storey hotel to boot. Gradually Bugsy turned it around and the business started to turn a profit. But it was perhaps too little too late. He was gunned down by an unknown shooter in June of the same year – shot multiple times through the window of his girlfriend's Beverly Hills home with an M1 carbine rifle, two .30 calibre rounds from the army-issue firearm striking him in the head and blowing his brains out. His murder remains unsolved, but a strong theory is that other factions of the US Mob, possibly led by Lucky Luciano, either believed Bugsy had been skimming profits from The Flamingo and not kicking back everything he should have been to his partners or had just run out of patience with their partner after the costs for The Flamingo had skyrocketed and it had struggled to turn a profit.

According to Campbell's account, Ronnie Kray had first flown into Chicago in the late 1960s to meet with Meyer Lansky. It seems the Mob's money man was more than happy for Ronnie to get a taste of what the US Mafia had going on in both Chicago and Las Vegas. For Ronnie, who was already working closely with Lansky and the Mob on their joint ventures in London, the Colony Sports Club included, it was a valuable research trip to see how they might be able to expand the scope and profitability of their UK operation.

By the time Ronnie Kray headed out to Las Vegas there were numerous hotels and casinos under the control of the US Mob, and Sin City had become one of the world's most glamorous destinations, hosting performers including members of the fabled Rat Pack like Frank Sinatra, Sammy Davis Jr. and Dean Martin.

In Las Vegas, Ronnie had been shown the Mob's Nevada operation. While there he had met Frank Sinatra – who had told him his son Frank Sinatra Jr. was about to travel to London for a series of live performances at The Palladium. Frank Sr. was worried his boy was at risk of being kidnapped while in the UK, and asked if Ronnie could help. Ronnie promised Ol' Blue Eyes he'd look after his son, and that the Krays would provide him with bodyguards. The exchange is less surprising, and much more believable, than many might think.

In December 1952 the seventh resort to open on The Strip in Las Vegas was The Sands Hotel and Casino. It would become one of the iconic venues of the Vegas of this era. Meyer Lansky was a shareholder, and before the end of 1953 had used his connections to lure Frank Sinatra into performing there. Before long, Sinatra himself was a shareholder. In 1960 it was a key location for the heist film *Ocean's 11*, starring Sinatra alongside his Rat Pack buddies Dean Martin, Sammy Davis Jr. and Peter Lawford – and featuring a cameo from a certain George Raft (who would also become a shareholder in The Sands). The Sands became the top Vegas hangout for the Rat Pack, and they were paid handsomely for performing at the hotel's famous Copa Room. Vegas in the 1950s and '60s was inextricably linked to the

US Mob, who clearly had an ongoing relationship with Sinatra and his pals.

It's perhaps unsurprising that Sinatra became so entwined with the American Mafia. He was born in Little Italy, Hoboken, to two first-generation Sicilian-American parents, in 1915. The city was the first to go 'dry' when Prohibition took effect in 1919 – and from then on the grip of organized crime never relented. Frank's dad Marty, a local prize fighter, became a guard on trucks running bootleg booze, and mum Dolly ran a saloon. From the very beginning Frank grew up surrounded by mobsters. Prohibition had made the US Mafia rich and powerful – and given them control of many of the country's bars and clubs. In fact, once Prohibition had ended it was his mum Dolly who got the teenage Frank his first proper break – she convinced her friend and Frank's godfather, the underboss of the New Jersey Genovese crime family Guarino 'Willie' Moretti, to give him a job in one of his clubs as long as he was allowed to sing a song or two. Soon he was travelling to Atlantic City as the vocalist for the Harry James band – and here he was introduced to another gangster friend of his mother's, the boss of the 500 Club and local legend Paul 'Skinny' D'Amato. Years later Skinny would partner with Frank on the Cal-Neva Lodge.

By the late 1940s the FBI were keeping tabs on the Mafia, and on Sinatra. The Bureau would keep him under surveillance for nearly five decades and amass a file on him amounting to over 2,400 pages. But their reports were kept secret by their director J. Edgar Hoover – who was being blackmailed by the Mob over his secret homosexuality. It was clear that Frank was keeping the company of, and singing for, some of the top men in American organized crime, including Lucky Luciano, Meyer Lansky, Bugsy Siegel, Albert Anastasia, Vito Genovese, Frank Costello and Joe Adonis – not least at the joint US and Italian Mafia's historic 1946 Havana Conference. His connections to the US Mob were undeniable. Even his second wife, movie star Ava Gardner, would go on to describe him as having been 'in bed with The Mob'.

Nowhere would this become more apparent than in Las Vegas – Sin City, the gambling capital of the country. Here Sinatra, known by many as the 'Chairman of the Board', was close friends with Jack Entratter – who ran The Sands, the hotel and casino part-funded by Meyer Lansky and featuring the Copa Room, a nightclub built especially for 'Ol' Blue Eyes' Sinatra himself. That was until Frank got his teeth knocked out at the casino by one of Entratter's lieutenants. By this point he had also been friends for many years with Chicago Mafia boss Sam 'Mooney' Giancana. Giancana had made a name for himself aged just 16, when he carried out an attempted hit on Chicago Mob boss Johnny Torrio on behalf of a certain Al Capone. He would later take part in Capone's infamous St Valentine's Day Massacre. And when Bugsy Siegel was killed, it was Giancana who stepped into the breach and took over the Chicago Mafia's interests in Hollywood. When Sinatra was down on his luck and worried his Mob ties might be exposed and ruin his career, it was Giancana who made sure Frank knew his secret was safe – as long as he agreed to perform in the Mafia-controlled clubs. It was a deal with the devil, but it seemingly saved Sinatra at the time.

As his career got back on track, Sinatra found himself bound ever more tightly to the Mob and to Giancana in particular. His resurgence had meant he had been able to become the part-owner of the Cal-Neva Lodge – a unique cross-border property that featured a hotel on the California side of the state line and a casino on the Nevada side. As I'd discovered, his fellow investor was 'Skinny' D'Amato. But Sinatra's silent partner in the business was none other than Sam Giancana, also known as 'Sam the Cigar'. Peter Lawford, one of Sinatra's close Rat Pack pals, even claimed 'My Kind of Town (Chicago Is)' was the singer's tribute to his Mob boss friend.

But eventually Sinatra would turn his back on Giancana, and distance himself from the Mob. Key to the change was the fate of the world's greatest sex symbol, and the hottest actress in Hollywood at the time, Marilyn Monroe. She and Frank had been lovers, but in the end he was forced to let her go – unwilling to stand between her and the man he had decided to throw his weight behind in the presidential race, John F. Kennedy. Sinatra was devastated when JFK, as soon as he had been inaugurated, took steps to distance himself from Frank and his alleged Mob ties. It was an understandable and perhaps shrewd political move, but Sinatra took it personally. JFK's administration and in particular his brother Robert F. Kennedy, the new attorney general, began a crusade against organized crime and the American Mafia in particular. It would have unforeseen and deadly consequences for them both.

Then on the morning of Sunday 5 August 1962, the news that Marilyn Monroe had died aged just 36 was broadcast across the country. Frank immediately questioned the official verdict of 'probable suicide' by barbiturate overdose. When he spoke to Ava on the phone she could tell that, although he never named him for fear his phone line was tapped, Frank suspected the involvement of Giancana and the Chicago Mob. From that moment on he turned against them – even going as far as to help Bobby Kennedy put Giancana behind bars. But the turning of the Kennedy brothers against the US Mafia would not go unpunished. JFK was assassinated in 1963. His brother Bobby was assassinated in 1968.

And, in the late '60s, when Ronnie Kray was visiting Las Vegas, it was still very much a Mob town. Ronnie was invited to a cocktail party at a huge Las Vegas mansion. On a tour of the property he was shown down into the substantial basement – only to find himself feet away from several fully grown tigers. They were behind bars, in a huge cage, but when he looked down Ronnie could see bloodstains all across the basement floor. Sensing his confusion, his host explained. The Mob's enemies would be brought down here and fed to the tigers. When the giant cats were finished with their grizzly meal, a 'bone collector' would come and take the remains and dispose of them at the Hoover Dam.

It's a chilling story if true. But given that, according to Campbell, Ronnie had flown to Chicago and then on to Las Vegas, perhaps this wasn't the same trip that ended in a narrow escape from a trial in Philadelphia alongside Philly crime family boss Angelo Bruno. But either way, it was intriguing – and was yet more possible evidence of links between the Krays and the US Mob, between Britain and the Mafia.

Chapter Eight

Boardwalk Empire,
The Atlantic City Story

———

Whenever Ronnie and his suitcase of cash did eventually get back on a plane to London – whether it was straight after his close call with the Philadelphia police and Angelo Bruno or if he sneaked in a quick recce in Las Vegas first before leaving the States – for the Philly Mob significant damage had still been done. Walking the streets of Philly, George Martorano told me how Bruno's arrest alongside Ronnie Kray had brought unwanted attention to the activities of the Gentle Don and the Philly Mob. Bruno feared the episode would put him on the radar not just of the FBI but of Interpol. He could see the writing on the wall. It might be easier to cut ties with Reggie and Ronnie, and with the London casino scene. Yes, London had proved to be a lucrative venture – and especially useful given its timing, with the legalization of gambling in the UK coming just months after the Mob's loss of their Havana casino operations thanks to Castro's victory in Cuba – but now there was a new great white gambling hope on the horizon that looked a lot more appealing than the complex transatlantic operation.

In 1976 a brand-new gambling licence was issued to create an exciting new destination for casinos and entertainment on America's east-coast waterfront. And it was right on Angelo Bruno's doorstep: Atlantic City, New Jersey.

This resort town had been so named in 1853. It had a direct train link to Philadelphia and a prime location on the Atlantic coastline. The city, and its famous boardwalk, grew in popularity. It was even the venue for the 1929 meeting at which Lucky Luciano and a group of criminal leaders from across the States founded the National Crime Syndicate. But in the post-war period the city struggled. It suffered from the national and global economic decline that followed the end of the Second World War, but also from the changing habits of the nation's holidaymakers. The popularity of the automobile meant many tourists now stayed at most for a few days in Atlantic City, rather than travelling in by train and staying a week. Others moved out to new, bigger suburban homes with gardens and pools and the draw of the boardwalk was lost. The rise of the passenger airplane opened up new, more exotic holiday destinations – suddenly South Jersey paled in comparison to Florida's Miami Beach or the Bahamas. As the 1960s ticked over into the 1970s many of the city's biggest hotels were struggling, suffering from low occupancy rates, and they began to close their doors for good. A 1974 referendum on legalizing gambling failed, but just two years later, with no signs of a return to their previous fortunes, the people of New Jersey voted to approve casino gambling in Atlantic City. On 26 May 1978 the first legal casino in the eastern United States, the Resorts Casino Hotel, opened its doors. Legalized gambling had seemed to be the last and perhaps only hope to revitalize the city – but it would have unforeseen repercussions. . .

The Philly family's interests in the Colony Sports Club in London might have netted them three to four million dollars a year, but controlling the gambling in Atlantic City could see them earn perhaps a hundred times that – three to four hundred million dollars a year, and without the need to extricate their funds from a foreign country. It wasn't long before Bruno severed all ties with the London casinos, the Colony Club included, and instead poured his efforts into gaining, and keeping, complete control of the operations in Atlantic City. It was a massive cash cow, and it was right on the Philly Mob's doorstep.

But this power came at a cost. Atlantic City became such a high-profile earner that it attracted the attention of Bruno's allies in the Five Families. They all wanted a piece of this golden goose, and felt it was unfair of Bruno to keep it all to himself. Atlantic City wasn't far from New York, after all.

George had stopped walking, and was standing next to me on the pavement, beside a red fire hydrant, when he told me that that was how Angelo Bruno 'wound up getting ambushed'. When I asked him where, he pointed over the road: 'Right across the street.' He had led me to the intersection of 10th Street and Snyder Avenue in the Lower Moyamensing neighbourhood of South

Philadelphia – a spot directly opposite the actual house where Philly Mafia boss Angelo Bruno had lived in the 1970s.

It was here, on this quiet street, where, on 21 March 1980, Angelo Bruno was shot dead. George told me that his godmother, Bruno's wife, was looking out of the upstairs window as the attack happened and screamed as her husband was gunned down. The 69-year-old Bruno was in the passenger seat of his car outside his house when he was blasted in the back of the head with a shotgun. He died instantly. His driver, John Stanfa, was injured, but survived the attack. Photos of the scene showed Bruno still sitting upright in the passenger seat, his head tilted back, eyes closed, the blood on his chin the same crimson red colour as his vehicle. As the authorities secured the scene, people lined the street to catch a glimpse of the slain Mob boss.

This brutal killing sent shockwaves through the Philly Mob. They knew they had to watch their backs. It led to a bloody four-year war for control of the turf. Not only that, it signalled the end of a generation of Mafia bosses. The Gentle Don and his like, the old-school godfathers who had focused on gambling and racketeering, were soon no more. They were to be replaced by a newer, younger, hungrier generation of Mafia boss. And the new guard were selling a new vice: drugs.

The neighbourhood George had been leading me through reflected back at me everything he had told me about Philly and about Angelo Bruno. It was a tough, poor part of town. As we walked and talked, and filmed, we were constantly approached by people – more often than not local men – who would ask us

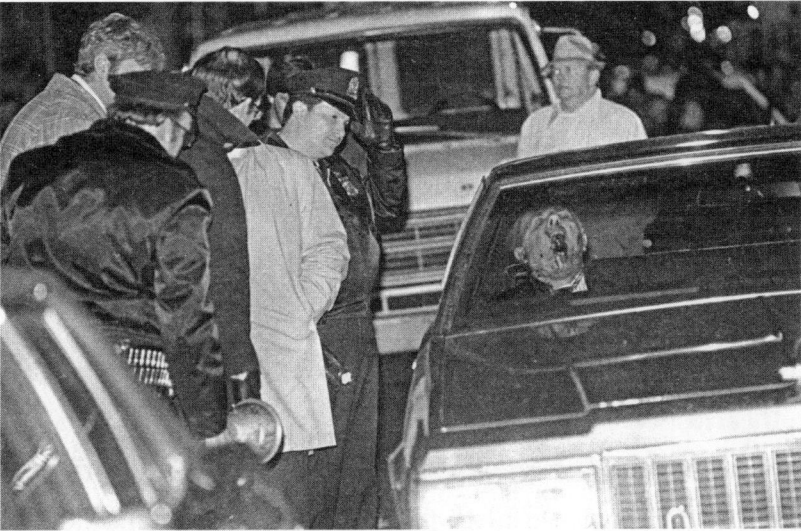

The body of Angelo Bruno, 'The Gentle Don', in the passenger seat of his car after being shot dead on 21 March 1980. Philadelphia police are checking the vehicle for clues.

somewhat leading questions about the cameras we were using. But many of them, when we told them we were filming an interview about Angelo Bruno, would immediately change their demeanour entirely. No sooner had we mentioned 'The Gentle Don' than they would proceed to tell us how much they missed Bruno, that he was the guy who 'made the neighbourhood work', that they loved him, that he looked out for the local people and that they were sad when he died. Angelo Bruno had been dead for more than 40 years and yet his memory lived on. And his was, from speaking to these regular people on the streets of Philly, a strangely positive legacy. It was clear he still loomed large over these streets even after all these years.

I was thinking about Bruno, the Philly Mob and the links to the UK, as the team sent up the drone to get some more aerial footage of the streets of the neighbourhood. And it was then that we had another close call – albeit this time a humorous one. We'd barely got the drone up into the sky before it came under attack. From a flock of pigeons. The birds' aerial assault corralled the drone in-between two sets of overhead cables, and we were running the very real risk of losing the drone or worse. A decision was taken and we brought the flying camera down immediately, before the situation got any more serious. Philly pigeons one, camera crew nil.

After this bizarre end to the day's filming we had a decision to make. We had a spare day before our next scheduled interview. Having heard so much about it and its role in ending the relationship between Angelo Bruno, the Philly Mob and the US Mafia and the London casino scene run by East End gangsters like the Krays and

Billy Hill, we decided on a day trip to Atlantic City – a location made famous by the TV drama series *Boardwalk Empire,* named after its most well-known landmark.

As we drove out of Philly the next day my head was filled with images of Atlantic City. I could just imagine the glitz and glamour, the bright lights of the 'Las Vegas of the East Coast' spilling out to the very shore of the Atlantic Ocean. The historic town, with its renowned boardwalk, felt like a quintessentially 'Mob' place to visit.

We drove out to the Jersey Shore, and headed south to Absecon Island. Here, on the barrier island's northern tip, sat the resort community of Atlantic City. My expectations were high. My imagination had been fired by the story of Prohibition-era racketeer and local bigwig Enoch L. 'Nucky' Johnson – the central character in *Boardwalk Empire.* In the 1920s he had risen to become the unofficial don of 'A.C.'. By then the city had grown, the seafront dominated by large hotels to cater to the hundreds of thousands of tourists who would visit every year to holiday by the sea, enjoy the now famous sweet, salty and chewy confectionery known as 'salt water taffy' and avail themselves of the free-flowing illegal alcohol on offer. The 19th-century seaside health resort had become a party town dubbed 'The World's Playground' – and central to it all was Nucky and his control of the illicit booze trade. With Prohibition barely enforced, Nucky was making half a million dollars a year from illegal liquor, gambling, prostitution and kickbacks on the numerous construction projects across town.

It was Nucky Johnson who had hosted, in Atlantic City, the 1929 conference of all the major organized crime heads from across

America, the event at which, during the meeting called by Lucky Luciano, the National Crime Syndicate had been created. It was on this very boardwalk that Al Capone had supposedly gone for a stroll with Nucky himself – if a well-known but hotly contested photograph is to be believed.

Nucky was born in New Jersey in 1883. His father, Smith E. Johnson, was a local sheriff, and Nucky soon followed in Dad's footsteps – he became his father's undersheriff in 1905 and in 1908, when Smith retired, Enoch was elected to replace him as sheriff of Atlantic County. He was also a key figure in the politics of Atlantic City, and in 1909 was elected as the committee secretary for the Atlantic County Republican Executive. This group controlled the city and was led by Louis 'Commodore' Kuehnle – the man responsible for turning the city into a thriving resort town. But Kuehnle's secret was to give the masses what they wanted, the three Bs: (illegal) booze, broads and blackjack – he was the man who ensured that A.C. allowed liquor, gambling and prostitution. In 1911 Kuehnle, Nucky and their colleagues were charged with corruption – but while Kuehnle was convicted, Nucky got off, and was able to succeed his boss as the most powerful man in Atlantic City.

While Nucky might not have been a Mafia man, he certainly lived the life of a godfather during Prohibition. Straddling the two worlds of legal and criminal, politician and gangster, his fortune and influence skyrocketed as he helped Atlantic City earn that nickname of 'The World's Playground'. Anyone serving alcohol or running a brothel or gambling den was protected as long as they kicked back a share of the profits to Nucky. Soon he was making nearly $10 million a year in today's money purely from his cut from every gallon of illegal liquor sold and from the city's thriving gambling and prostitution businesses.

Safe to revel in his wealth – he was no secretive Mob boss but in fact the very public face of the city – he wore a $1,200 raccoon fur coat and was driven around in a $14,000 powder-blue limousine. His personal trademark was a freshly cut red carnation worn on his lapel. He lived right on the city's famous boardwalk, in a suite on the ninth floor of the Ritz-Carlton Hotel. Known as both 'the Czar of the Ritz' and 'the Prisoner of the Ritz', he was famous for hosting lavish parties. And, ever the politician, he also made sure to share just enough of his wealth and generosity with the local population, and with those in need – ensuring he was well loved by his citizens. That element of his story reminded me of how the men on the street of Philly had spoken of Angelo Bruno and of the years of the 'Gentle Don'.

The repeal of Prohibition in 1933 was the beginning of the end for Nucky and the start of a long, slow decline for Atlantic City. In 1939 he was indicted for evading taxes on over $100,000 he had made from numbers operators in the mid-1930s. He finally went to trial in 1941, was found guilty and was sentenced to ten years in federal prison and fined $20,000. On 11 August 1941, Nucky entered Lewisburg Federal Penitentiary.

In 1945, following his early release on parole, and with A.C. devastated by the war years and the 1944 Great Atlantic Hurricane, the city was already on the slide. To avoid paying a hefty $20,000 fine, as part of the conditions of his freedom Nucky took the 'pauper's oath' – and from then until his death in 1968 he lived a much more subdued and simple life, albeit he continued to sport a bright red carnation in his lapel.

Atlantic City was steeped in Mob history. First for its original golden age in the 1920s and 1930s – when the boardwalk had been 7 miles long, when it was the home of the Miss America pageant (for over 80 years, from its very first competition in 1921), when its streets had been the basis for the original Parker Brothers 1935 edition of Monopoly and when Nucky had ruled over it all. But then latterly for the casino boom of the late 1970s and beyond that I had recently learned so much about – the era of 'The Gentle Don' Angelo Bruno.

This period of major US Mob involvement in Atlantic City coincided with the legalization of gambling in the town. When, on 26 May 1978, the ribbon was cut at the opening of the Resorts Atlantic City hotel and casino, A.C. had America's first legal casino outside the state of Nevada. Many others would follow. In June 1977, when he had signed into law the bill permitting casino gambling in Atlantic City, New Jersey Governor Brendan Byrne had declared: 'Organized crime is not welcome in Atlantic City. I warn them – keep your filthy hands out of Atlantic City. Keep the hell out of our state.'

But Angelo Bruno and the Philly Mob had no intention of heeding his words. They made sure they got their piece of the pie. They didn't even wait for the construction of the first casino to be completed. An article published by the *New York Times* on

5 February 1978 claimed their extensive investigations had already uncovered attempts by members and associates of organized crime families to 'invest in Atlantic City real estate, bars, restaurants, motels, croupiers' schools, casino hotels, a jewellery store, a janitorial company and an airport'. By the time of Bruno's death in 1980 the US Mafia were firmly entrenched in this new 'Gambling Capital of the East Coast' – and as I now knew, that meant they had been able to withdraw from their dealings with the East End gangsters running London's casinos.

I was aware that the years in-between the two golden eras under first Nucky Johnson in the 1920s of Prohibition and then Angelo Bruno in the late 1970s and early '80s, especially the period from 1944 to 1978, had been extremely tough for Atlantic City – but I was excited to take in the sights, sounds and smells of this Jersey Vegas, to breathe in its Mob history and to experience the old-school glitz and glamour.

Unfortunately, I was to be deeply disappointed. I had hoped that a city that had seen that much investment over decades of the 20th century, even if it had been thanks to organized crime, would be a sight to behold even today. But as we drove by row upon row of derelict buildings, past street corners populated by swathes of the homeless and impoverished, instead of glitz and glamour, or even the frisson of excitement from a bustling town with an edgy reputation, all I got was an abiding sense of the misery of the place. It was poor. It was down at heel. It had a huge problem with drug addiction, crime and homelessness. It was depressing. It was comparable to some seaside towns back in the UK that had also seen their fair share of tough times over the years, but on a massive scale.

The one exception, unsurprisingly, was the boardwalk. This seaside promenade, and the strip of hotels and casinos along it, still held remnants of the glory of yesteryear. But it was a glimmering island in a sea of poverty, crime and destitution. On the drive back I found myself saddened by the plight of the city and – perhaps for the first time on this journey into Britain's links with the Mafia – disappointed by what I had seen and learned.

Thankfully, this wasn't the end of the line. I knew that tomorrow I would be off again on the trail of the UK's links to the most historic and famous organized crime groups in the world.

Chapter Nine

Drugs: Cocaine, The New Scourge

———

When we had been walking the streets of Philly, George had told me that he and his fellow Philly mobsters had had plenty of experience dealing cannabis by the bucketload, and that this revenue stream at the softer end of the drugs trade was bringing them in a lot of cash, in fact more than they had ever made before. But as the 1970s were ending, the US drug market was shifting away from weed and towards what he referred to as 'powder' – heroin. George had never dealt with these harder drugs, but he knew of Italian mobsters up in Harlem, New York, who were making millions dealing powder. And by the late 1970s this was the norm. Making millions from dealing heroin was what George succinctly called 'playing the game'. And the American Mafia dons running this hard drugs operation were increasingly brutal and violent.

The creation of Atlantic City in the mid-1970s might have seen the US Mob's old guard sever ties with London's casino scene, but did the growing drugs business stateside lead to a rekindling of a Mafia relationship with Britain? I met with someone that might help me find out: Mafia expert Professor Antonio Nicaso.

Antonio is one of the world's leading authorities on the Mafia's international networks. He told me how the US Mob were the creators of one of the most significant criminal enterprises in the history of organized crime: the first international heroin pipeline. And soon they were making billions of dollars on both sides of the ocean.

Illegal and highly addictive, heroin was a key commodity for the US Mafia families and a highly profitable part of their criminal empires. But the opium needed for its production came from well-established poppy plantations in Afghanistan.

Poppy fields used to produce opium may have been encouraged in Afghanistan at the end of the 19th century, when it had fallen under British control following the Second Anglo-Afghan War. Britain had long been active in the growth of poppy plantations and the opium trade, even going to war with China over the trade in the two 'Opium Wars' of the mid-19th century. But the 1950s saw a major expansion – as Afghanistan pivoted to fill the void left when neighbour Iran banned the cultivation of the poppy. By the mid-1970s Afghanistan had become one of the word's biggest suppliers of opiates.

To exploit the American market fully, the Mafia knew they would need to bring the resources of its international network to bear. If they could control the heroin trade into the US they knew they would have won the jackpot. And so a plan was devised between the Sicilian Mafia and their cousins in America, the

US Mob. This new transatlantic partnership pooled their resources to purchase large quantities of raw opium directly from Afghanistan and Pakistan. They shipped it to Sicily, where it was refined in Mafia labs, and then transported it on to America, where the US Mob could oversee distribution.

But it was at this point in his explanation that Antonio told me something that really got my attention. He revealed that the Sicilian Mafia group overseeing the shipments of tonnes of heroin from the Italian island to the United States – the Cuntrera and Caruana families – decided the best way to get the drugs across the Atlantic was via the UK. And they had already planted operatives in Britain to help establish this new heroin transportation hub in London as early as the 1970s. When I asked Antonio if he knew where this member of the Caruana family was based, his answer stopped me in my tracks: Woking. I was so surprised I had to clarify. 'Woking? Woking, Surrey? Are you kidding me?' I could barely believe that a Mafia associate tasked with overseeing the transportation of huge volumes of heroin between Sicily, the UK and the US could have been living in this commuter town just to the west of London.

And then Antonio dropped a second bombshell. He revealed that another Sicilian mobster joined the Cuntrera-Caruana operation in London: Francesco Di Carlo. This was a name that I knew well, none other than Frankie the Strangler, the hitman initially suspected of the murder of Roberto Calvi, God's Banker. Now it seemed that Di Carlo might actually have been in the UK to oversee the Mafia's heroin pipeline. Antonio explained that Frankie the Strangler was the mastermind of the operation – shipping billions of dollars of hashish and heroin to England hidden in Italian furniture and then sending it on to North America.

And it wasn't just drug trafficking in which the Mafia were involved in the UK in the 1970s. London, the country's financial capital, was also their preferred money laundering destination. The Cuntrera-Caruanas perceived themselves as bankers, and became known as the Rothschilds of the Mafia – so plentiful were the proceeds of Mafia crimes that they were washing in the merchant banks of London.

By the end of the 1970s the New York Mob were selling heroin that had come through this new pipeline, from Afghanistan, Thailand and Turkey to Sicily, and then on to the USA – often via the UK, in pizza boxes. The Italian-American influx into the US had created one of the 20th century's greatest culinary inventions – the American pizza pie. In the '70s the Mob, predominantly the Bonanno family, the most Sicilian of the US crime families, began buying up pizza parlours. These cash businesses, with a built-in delivery network and infrastructure, were the perfect front for laundering Mafia money – and delivering drugs. Between 1975 and 1984 it's estimated that the Sicilian Mafia sent 1,650lbs of heroin – with a street value of $1.6 billion – from Palermo to the Bonanno's pizza parlours in New York City. The drug could be delivered to the restaurants alongside their food supplies, sent to customers using branded delivery vehicles, passed over hidden in pizza boxes and the proceeds laundered through the company's accounts. It was a criminal enterprise brilliant in its simplicity – and became known as 'The Pizza Connection'.

But this boom time for heroin was relatively short lived. With the arrival of the 1980s came the arrival on the global crime scene of a new player in the game, with a new product to shift. Pablo Escobar had risen to become the cocaine king of Colombia. His Medellín Cartel's ability to mass-produce and supply this drug led to an explosion in demand for the white powder across the United States, which was much more socially acceptable than heroin. Coke became the go-to party drug for the rich and famous, and a key part of the aspirations of a generation of Americans. The popularity of cocaine in the '80s changed the face of organized crime for ever.

This new cocaine trade also had an impact on the criminal centres of the United States. Initially it was Miami, not New York, as was the case with heroin, that became the key hub for the drug in the US. Miami was closer to Colombia, it was the nearest major US port to the country, and it was here that the Medellín Cartel focused their product. The US Mob was shifting its focus – from heroin supplied by their Italian Mafia counterparts and shipped from Europe to New York, to cocaine supplied to Miami by the new kids on the block, the Colombian cartels.

It was clear where I needed to go next: Florida. We dropped off the hire car at Philadelphia International Airport, and headed inside – only to quickly discover there was a problem. Our flight down to Miami was delayed. We waited. And then we waited some more. And some more. We were there for hours before we were finally able to board a plane. Travel delays come with the territory, but when you're working to a tight schedule they can be costly in more ways than one – and I was desperate to get down to Miami in a bid to uncover what links the centre of the US cocaine trade might have forged between the US Mafia and Britain.

When I was finally driving my rental car along Ocean Drive it all felt a million miles away from the faded glory of Atlantic City, the mean streets of Philly and especially from the cold walk along the foreshore of the Thames that had begun my journey. I was down here in the glorious Florida sunshine to find out how the East Coast Mob all the way up in New York had become involved with the millions of tonnes of Colombian cocaine that were flooding into Miami thanks to Pablo Escobar and the Medellín Cartel. The man who could help me make sense of this tactical shift was Anthony Ruggiano Jr. – a former Mafia associate who was based in the city in the 1980s. I met him on a sunny Miami pavement, and as we walked and talked he gave me the background.

Miami had only been incorporated as a city in 1896, thanks to the efforts of the only woman to found a major US city – Julia Tuttle. It's strategic importance as a naval base during the Second World War saw its population grow to over 170,000 by 1940. And it expanded still further with a significant influx of Cuban refugees following Castro's victory in 1959. By 1980 Miami's population was just under 350,000 – and it was already a 'majority-minority' city, with over 55 per cent of the population Latino or Hispanic, and under 20 per cent 'white'.

In the early 1980s Miami was far from the city it is today. It was cocaine money that helped build it. Anthony remembered the Colombians would hold court in beautiful apartments, with armed guards in the halls and prostitutes at their beck and call.

They would cook the cocaine right there in the apartment. It was a bloody and brutal period of Miami's history. At the time, the East Coast Mob had next to no influence in Miami, but it wasn't long before what was happening there got their attention. In 1985 New York's Gambino family sent Anthony's father, a made member of the Mob, down to Florida. As they had done in Las Vegas, in Atlantic City, and even in London, the US Mob – despite their predominantly New York power base – were once again expanding their operation. It was a Mafia trademark that dated back to the very inception of the organization in Italy hundreds of years earlier – follow the money, muscle in and take control.

Anthony's father opened up a restaurant in Miami: Danno's. The spot in North Bay Village soon became a hub for Colombians and Cubans, and their American Mafia counterparts, to manage the cocaine trade. Anthony's father would move from table to table, drink in hand, as his Latin American patrons made calls on their giant satellite phones. And it wasn't just the Gambinos, or even the Five Families, who were doing business with the Colombians. Anthony told me that there were 'wise guys' from New Orleans, Buffalo, Chicago and more. They were all moving large quantities of Colombian cocaine from Florida all the way up the Eastern seaboard.

And, as Anthony explained, moving the coke further north was of huge financial benefit. In the early '80s a gram of cocaine in Miami might sell for $40. But at a club in New York like the infamous Studio 54 that same gram might go for $120. Miami was a gold mine – giving the US Mob a vast supply of Colombian cocaine that they could distribute into their East Coast territories for a huge mark-up. The cocaine trade in Florida was soon worth around $12 billion a year.

Anthony, like many of those involved in the coke business, was using – getting high on his own supply. He told me he liked it, but it took him to a dark, violent place. I could see in his eyes a hint of some of the darkness he was reliving as he spoke to me. I was reminded that he was, like so many of the other men I had met so far, a hardened criminal. He also told me that many of Miami's police were corrupt, were taking money from the gangsters and getting rich in the process, and would even give police escorts to the Colombian narcos to make sure they got away cleanly. He also told me about a police unit crew that went rogue and became dealers themselves. In 1984 these Miami police officers began to seize and then steal drugs and cash taken from local criminals stopped for traffic violations. As their network of informants and criminal contacts grew, the cops used the tip-offs they were getting from their sources to target their off-book raids on sizeable drug stashes. Their operations came to a head in July 1985. In a raid on the *Mitzi Ann*, a boat docked at the Tamiami Marina, they seized hundreds of kilograms of cocaine that had been secreted in hidden compartments within the vessel. Then they hit the *Mary C* – a pleasure boat at the Jones Boat Yard on the Miami River. This time they got around 350 kilograms of coke, with a street value of $10 million, which they drove off with in a van. But in this raid three of the criminal crew who had been attempting to unload the drugs fell into the river and drowned while trying to make their escape. They had heard the Hispanic officers shouting, *'¡Matarlos! ¡Matarlos!'* ('Kill them! Kill them!') And unfortunately for the corrupt cops, these bodies were found. An investigation was opened into what had gone on at the boat yard. And when undercover cops caught their corrupt colleagues trying to sell the drugs they had snatched from the *Mary C* and *Mitzi Ann*, the game was up. Seven Miami police officers were arrested and faced trial – and became known as the River Cops. The initial proceedings resulted in a mistrial, but a second trial indicted twenty officers – including the original seven. Eventually one of the accused turned state's evidence – becoming a witness for the prosecution. This resulted in ten of the accused pleading guilty – and two being found guilty at a trial in February 1988.

As the trade in Miami had grown, more and more mobsters and criminals had flocked to this Florida cocaine gold rush. I asked Anthony if he knew of anyone I could try to speak to who had been directly involved in the coke business here in Miami in those days. A British tourist passing by recognized me and came over to say hello – and when I had finished talking to them, Anthony told me that yes, there was one guy, named Dominick, from the Bronx, who he thought had later become a captain in the Bonanno family. Anthony said this Dominick was involved in drug trafficking. So, before Anthony and I parted ways, I asked him to see if he could connect me with Dominick. Before I left he gave me a number. I was in luck. I was able to make contact with Dominick – and he was prepared to speak to me. We hastily pulled together a plan, and I was soon walking down a sunny alley in Miami on my way to meet him.

Chapter Ten

The Fall of The Mob

———

I could see a man in the distance, a big guy in a bright red T-shirt, standing in the shadows at the side of the alley. It was hot, so perhaps he was just taking advantage of what little shade there was to stay cool. He stepped into the sunlight to greet me and shook my hand. As we sat on a wall and talked I was struck by the physical presence of the man I now knew was Dominick Cicale, a former Mafia captain. As rollerbladers sped past us, oblivious, Dominick told me that he had in fact been affiliated with the Genovese crime family, but that he hadn't answered to anyone. He had just done his own thing. He was a lone wolf. And he had been lured in by Miami. As he said, 'I wanted it. I wanted the money, the glitz, the glamour, the glory.'

But Dominick wasn't a dealer. He was a takedown merchant – robbing dealers of their coke and cash. Stealing from criminals has one major advantage: they're never going to report the crime to the authorities. And cocaine was the perfect drug to target – as even small quantities were worth a lot. Before Dominick was even out of his teens he estimated he was a self-made Mafia millionaire, having made over a million dollars from robbing Miami's drug dealers and stash houses and selling any coke he snatched for a big profit back home in the Big Apple.

But soon Dominick was operating in the middle of a war zone. In the 1980s Miami was a battleground, as rival Mafia groups, Colombian cartels and dealers fought over their patches and for the control of cocaine in and out of the city. The murder rate was astronomical, with hundreds of murders – often over 500 – every year. Since 1981 the city morgue had been forced to operate beyond its capacity and was renting out a refrigerated truck in which to store the surplus of cadavers that were flooding in daily. One woman was suspected of involvement in tens, if not hundreds, of the murders that took place in the late 1970s and early 1980s – Pablo Escobar's infamous Miami associate Griselda Blanco.

Ms Blanco is someone many of you might be familiar with thanks to the recent eponymous scripted drama series *Griselda*, starring the fabulous Colombian actress Sofia Vergara of *Modern Family* fame. Her story is a sidebar, not directly related to my investigation into the links between the Mafia in both Italy and the US and the UK – but it serves to perfectly illustrate the state of Miami in the 1980s, exactly when Dominick and many other gangsters, criminals and chancers from across the USA, including from the Five Families up in New York and the New Jersey Mob, were looking to muscle in on the explosion of the cocaine trade that Pablo and the Medellín Cartel had opened up in Florida.

Griselda Blanco was born in 1943 in Cartagena, on Colombia's Caribbean coast, but moved to Medellín when she was only three.

She grew up in Colombia's second city in the 1950s, and began to cultivate a criminal career at a similar time and in a not too dissimilar vein to her future partner Pablo Escobar. At age 11 she had been part of a gang that had kidnapped a rich young boy from Medellín. Blanco had ended up shooting him dead when the family didn't immediately pay the ransom.

In 1964 Griselda Blanco divorced her first husband Carlos Trujillo, a criminal, hustler and cannabis dealer – although the couple continued to do business together until they eventually fell out over a drugs deal and Griselda had him killed. Not long after, she relocated to New York. Here, with her young family (three boys, Dixon, Uber and Osvaldo, all from her relationship with Trujillo) and her new husband – Medellín Cartel member Alberto Bravo – she founded a flourishing drugs empire. In Queens she was able to work alongside the Five Families, importing high quality Colombian cocaine direct to New York. But in 1975 an indictment on federal drug conspiracy charges, part of 1974's Operation Banshee – launched by the brand-new DEA – saw the family flee back to Colombia to avoid prosecution. It wasn't long before the married couple fell out – and Blanco killed her second husband, shooting him in the face with her pistol as he returned fire with an Uzi. Six bodyguards were killed in the chaotic shootout in the car park of a Bogotá nightclub. Griselda was badly wounded, shot in the stomach, but survived – and gained a new nickname: 'the Black Widow'.

In the aftermath of the murder of Bravo, she returned to America – but this time to Miami. And it was here, in the Florida sunshine, that she created and oversaw one of the most crucial parts of the growing global cocaine pipeline that saw the Colombian cartels exporting the drug to the USA in huge quantities. She married for a third time, and the couple named their son Michael Corleone – after the character from the most famous book and film ever made about the Italian Mafia: *The Godfather*. When her third husband, Darío Sepúlveda, left her, returned to Colombia and had Michael kidnapped and brought back to live with him, it was only a matter of time.

In 1983, Darío was living with Michael in Medellín, Colombia, hoping to shield his son from Griselda's life of crime and violence in Miami and to dodge her wrath himself. It was a vain hope. Reports claim Darío was driving with his son when he was pulled over by what he thought were police. The men, dressed as police officers, asked him to get out of the car and immediately put handcuffs on him. Realizing something was badly wrong, Sepúlveda turned and ran. The men gunned him down as his son Michael looked on from inside the car. The young boy got out of the vehicle and ran over to his father, but he was already dead. It is believed that the killers were working for Blanco, although she has never been charged with any involvement in his death and to this day her son Michael maintains he cannot believe she was responsible.

Whatever the truth, Griselda Blanco's fourth son was soon back with her in Miami.

By this point she had become known as a ruthless operator – and, in a nod to the traditions of the Italian Mafia that had spread across the criminal world, was dubbed '*La Madrina*',

Roberto Calvi, the man known as 'God's Banker', during an investigation by Italian police in 1982 – the year of his death.

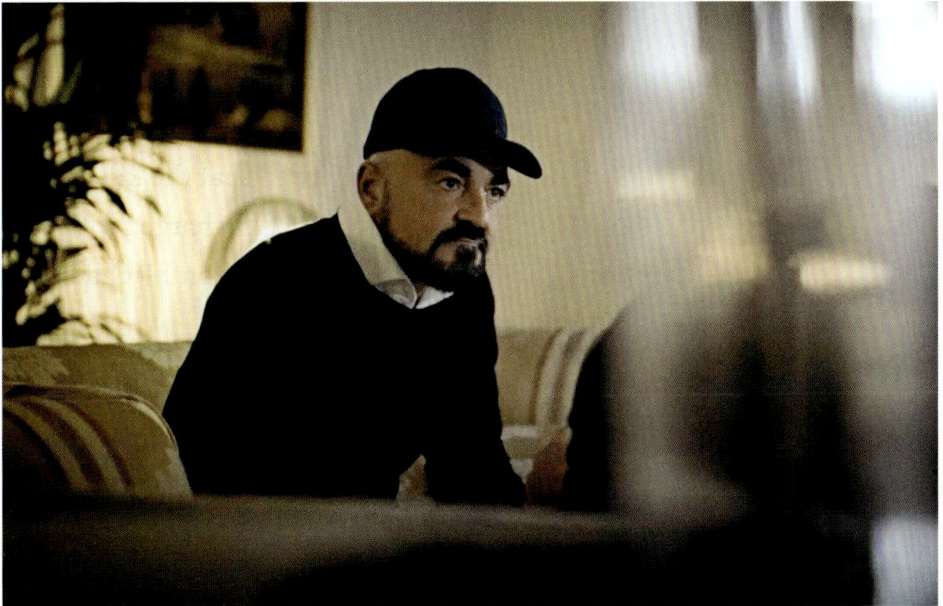

Former Preston resident Gennaro Panzuto, at an undisclosed location in his home city of Naples for our interview.

Charles 'Lucky' Luciano (centre) enjoying a drink during a news conference at Rome's Excelsior Hotel on 11 June 1948.

The Kray twins, Ronnie (left) and Reggie (right), at home in London in 1966.

The 'Godfather of London' Billy Hill (centre), pictured with associates at a London bar on 1 August 1954.

Angelo Bruno in New Jersey, 16 June 1977. Just three years later, the 'Gentle Don' of the Philly Mob would be shot dead aged 69.

Henry Hill in 2005, slicing pizza in the Nebraska restaurant kitchen where he worked. Hill's life and Mob exploits were dramatized by Martin Scorsese in the 1990 film *Goodfellas*.

Walking the streets of Philadelphia with former Philly Mob member George 'Cowboy' Martorano.

Chatting with Salvatore 'Crazy Sal' Polisi in Queens, New York. The former associate of the Colombo and Gambino crime families was thrilled at the chance to tell me his tales of the old days.

Owney Madden, pictured leaving the district attorney's office in New York City. His violent reputation earned him his nickname, 'The Killer'.

John Joseph Gotti Jr. (centre), head of the Gambino family, leaving Manhattan Supreme Court on 8 January 1990. He was on trial for charges of conspiracy and assault.

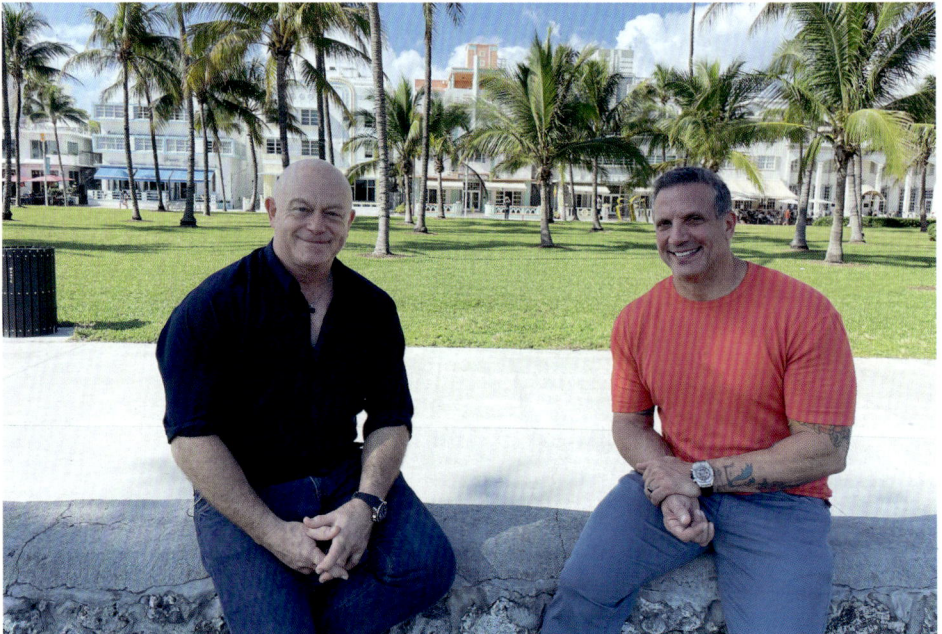

All smiles in sunny Miami with former Mafia captain and convicted killer Dominick Cicale.

Kitted out and in action with the Apolo special operations unit in Colombia. That night we would set off on a dangerous raid deep into the Cauca Valley, on the hunt for active cocaine laboratories.

Jesus Ruiz-Henao, speaking to me via video call from Bogotá's high-security La Picota prison.

Brit Charlie Wilson, of Great Train Robbery fame.

Notorious crime lord Emilio Di Giovine (left) and his daughter
Marisa Merico (right), during my interview with them at
Marisa's home in Lancashire.

'The Godmother'. Her trademark was using a network of young, often glamorous Colombian women – brought over from the brothels and clubs of her homeland to Miami – to import and distribute her product, supplied by Pablo and the Medellín Cartel. She even used her friend Maria Gutierrez, a struggling local Miami travel agent, to book all the flights for the girls, the *mulas* – drug mules. She bought an underwear business, had the garments adapted with secret pockets and pouches fitted, and had her mulas use them to walk off the planes from Colombia with cocaine strapped beneath their clothes. And as she rose to rule the Miami cocaine scene, trafficking some 300 kilograms of coke a month and becoming a multi-millionaire in the process, the murder rate in the city spiked and the period known as the Miami drug war began. She had gathered a group of gunmen around her – her *pistoleros* – and they waged war on the streets of Miami, gunning down rivals from their motorbikes at point-blank range and bringing their mistress back a severed body part to confirm the kill. They were responsible for the 1979 shopping centre shootout that became known as the Dadeland Massacre, a spectacular drive-by attack that kicked off the Miami drug war. It's believed Griselda Blanco was directly responsible for ordering tens, probably hundreds, of killings as this conflict raged. One estimate suggested she might have had at least 250 bodies on her ledger.

In 1985 The Godmother was arrested by DEA agents 2,500 miles west of Miami, where she was lying low in a suburban bungalow in Irvine, California. La Madrina was charged with conspiracy to manufacture, import and distribute cocaine. She was found guilty at a federal court in New York City and sentenced to 15 years – albeit to be served at FCI Dublin, a low-security federal prison for female offenders. A subsequent case brought by the state of Florida, charging her with three counts of first-degree murder, collapsed when the prosecution's star witness – Blanco's trusted hitman Jorge 'Rivi' Ayala – was found to have engaged in phone sex with a secretary from the state attorney's office. In the end Blanco pleaded guilty in 1998 to second-degree murder. But in 2002 she suffered a heart attack in prison, and in 2004 was finally released on compassionate grounds. She was allowed to return to Colombia, where she lived back in Medellín until in 2012, aged 69, she was shot twice in the head by a motorbike-riding assassin as she walked out of a local butcher's shop with her pregnant daughter-in-law. It was an act that mimicked one of her preferred methods of killing as practised during the Miami drug war all those years earlier.

During the early 1980s, as cocaine from Medellín flooded into Miami and Griselda Blanco and her friends and rivals took control of the drugs trade in the city, the DEA, the FBI, the Miami police and successive US administrations struggled to keep a lid on the Florida powder keg. And my interviewee Dominick found himself in what he felt was a kill or be killed situation as the Miami drug war raged around him. He had arranged for some of his friends to rob a drug dealer. But the very next day the dealer called him up and told him he knew he was behind it. Dominick denied it, but the dealer wasn't convinced. He offered someone $20,000 to kill Dominick. But unbeknownst to him, the hired gun was in fact one of Dominick's father's friends. Later that same night the friend told Dominick all about the offer he had been made to kill him, and together the pair made a plan. They lured the dealer into the friend's motel room. When the dealer walked into the room Dominick appeared, pushed him against the wall and held a gun to his head. The guy bolted for the doorway, and Dominick shot him in the back of the head. Twice.

I wasn't quite sure what to say, but Dominick's story didn't end there. He went on to tell me how the two men got cleaning materials, cleaned up the crime scene, wrapped up the body and took it down from the third-floor motel room to the trunk of a car and then drove it out to Palm Beach County. The corpse wasn't found for a month.

The cool, calm, matter-of-fact way Dominick relayed the story of this brutal murder left me in no doubt: this guy was a stone-cold killer. He may have been charged with two murders during his time with the Mafia, but Dominick justified the killings to which he freely admitted by explaining to me that the people whose lives he took were all 'part of the life'. As he said to me: 'These are guys who would kidnap kids. . . they would kill me in a heartbeat if they had the opportunity.' But Dominick didn't get away with his crimes. He was hit with a murder charge and was facing the death penalty, or at the very least life in prison. So, when he told me his lawyers helped him secure a plea deal that would mean he only had to serve 17 months, I almost fell off the wall. I was sitting opposite a man who had shot a man twice in the head, murdered him – in fact, murdered at least one other person – and had spent less than a year and a half behind bars for his crimes.

As we drove with Dominick to our next location we got lost in the maze of Miami's streets. The look he gave my executive producer, who was the poor unfortunate behind the wheel, was not one I will forget. When they say 'if looks could kill' they could have been talking about this guy. I think we were all glad that when we did actually get a flat tyre while driving through Miami Dominick was not with us in the car!

Thankfully, we eventually found our way and minutes later, as we sat at a low wooden table on the patio of a simple South Florida home, Dominick revealed that he had ended up serving a much longer sentence, but for a much lesser crime. Not long after he got out of prison, he was caught by the DEA taking part in a low-level drugs transaction, but was convicted of conspiracy to distribute for his part in a 2–3 kilogram cocaine deal. He was sentenced to ten years, and served nine of them. This strong sentence was part of a message being sent from the very top of the governments of both the United States and the United Kingdom. This was the 'War on Drugs' – led by the administrations of US President Ronald Reagan and British Prime Minister Margaret Thatcher. The idea of the war on drugs had begun during the Vietnam War and the administration of Richard Nixon. But it was given a new lease of life, and new focus, with the arrival of Ronald Reagan in the White House in 1981.

While the US went after the Mob in New York, cracked down on cocaine in Miami and helped the Colombian government wage war on Pablo Escobar and the Medellín Cartel, in the UK the focus was on smashing the heroin trade. The British government believed they were making progress, pressuring Pakistan and Afghanistan to reduce their trade in heroin.

Closer to home, the Cuntrera-Caruana clan, elements of which I now knew had been based in Woking, had their smuggling pipeline dismantled by international law enforcement. They had first come to the attention of the authorities outside Italy during initial investigations into the so-called Pizza Connection investigation. Then, in 1985, a joint operation between the Royal Canadian Mounted Police (RCMP) and British Customs and Excise seized heroin transports in London and Montreal. Subsequent investigations uncovered a key Cuntrera-Caruana heroin supply route from Thailand. In 1988 the RCMP seized a 30 kilogram shipment of heroin at a factory in Windsor, Ontario – just across the Detroit River from America. The same year, two key members of the family were arrested in Germany – where the German Bundeskriminalamt (BKM) – the country's federal police – uncovered an extensive Cosa Nostra network intent on setting up a heroin trafficking route from the Far East to mainland Europe.

But in the US, the primary target was the cocaine trade. I made some calls, and arranged to meet a man with first-hand knowledge of just how America sought to fight the tide of cocaine that was engulfing the nation.

In a quiet bar, I pulled up a stool next to Michael McGowan. The retired FBI special agent, in a weathered leather bomber jacket, flat cap pulled low, a magnificent silver moustache gracing his top lip, told me how the cocaine epidemic had been out of control. He joined the FBI in 1987, when cocaine was everywhere, the Mob was at the height of its power, and law enforcement in the US was just 'putting our fingers in the dyke, trying to stop it'. Then the FBI was tasked with getting a grip on the situation. Their primary target? The group behind the nationwide distribution of cocaine, and the primary domestic dealers of the drug. The Feds were going after the Mob. At the top of the FBI's list was the head of the Gambino family, John Gotti.

John Joseph Gotti Jr. was born in the New York City borough of the Bronx on 27 October 1940. His parents too were born in New York but had married in San Giuseppe Vesuviano, just outside Naples, and had lived there for some time – presumably with his Neapolitan grandparents. Aged 12, John was living in poverty with his family in East New York, Brooklyn, and was already getting involved with local street gangs who had links to mafiosi. He dropped out of school at 16, and before long was running errands for a capo in the Anastasia Mafia crime family – later to be the Gambino family. Soon he graduated to hijacking trucks. After three arrests, he was finally sent to prison for the first time. As he worked his way up within the Mafia, Gotti impressed his peers and those above him – he wasn't just tough, he was smart and charismatic. He also served yet more time inside on behalf of the family, for his part in the murder of the man who had killed the nephew of the new boss Carlo Gambino, Emanuel 'Manny' Gambino. Gotti and his alleged accomplices, Angelo 'Quack Quack' Ruggiero and Ralph 'Ralphie Wigs' Galione, attempted the abduction of the target – James 'Jimmy' McBratney – at Snoope's, a Staten Island bar. They were disguised as detectives, but

McBratney smelled a rat and tried to bolt. Gotti and Ruggiero grabbed him and held him still while Galione shot him dead. The crime-scene photograph has become infamous: a man lying spread-eagled on the floor of the bar, white shoes, black socks, his shirt and undershirt pulled up revealing a hairy beer belly, the fly of his trousers open wide as if he had been shot while urinating. It was an ignominious end for McBratney, and a stepping stone for Gotti on his rise to the top.

However, Gotti was identified by an eyewitness and arrested. But a plea bargain saw him serve just four years on a charge of 'attempted manslaughter'. In the end, Carlo Gambino actually died while Gotti was in prison – but on his release, the man anointed as Gambino's successor, Paul Castellano, immediately brought John into the family and promoted him to capo. John's crew quickly became the family's top earners. Gotti even played a major role in the infamous Lufthansa Heist at JFK. But growing increasingly disgruntled with Castellano's leadership, not least his stance against his men dealing in drugs, Gotti decided to take out his boss. On 16 December 1985 he finally got his chance, and his men assassinated Castellano at the Sparks Steak House on East 46th Street in Midtown Manhattan. Just weeks later his fellow capos voted him in as the new boss, despite everyone knowing he was the man behind the hit on Castellano. Gotti was the new don of the Gambino family, which was the most powerful of the Five Families at the time. The family was bringing in $500 million a year, and Gotti himself was taking somewhere between $5 million and $12 million a year now that he was in charge.

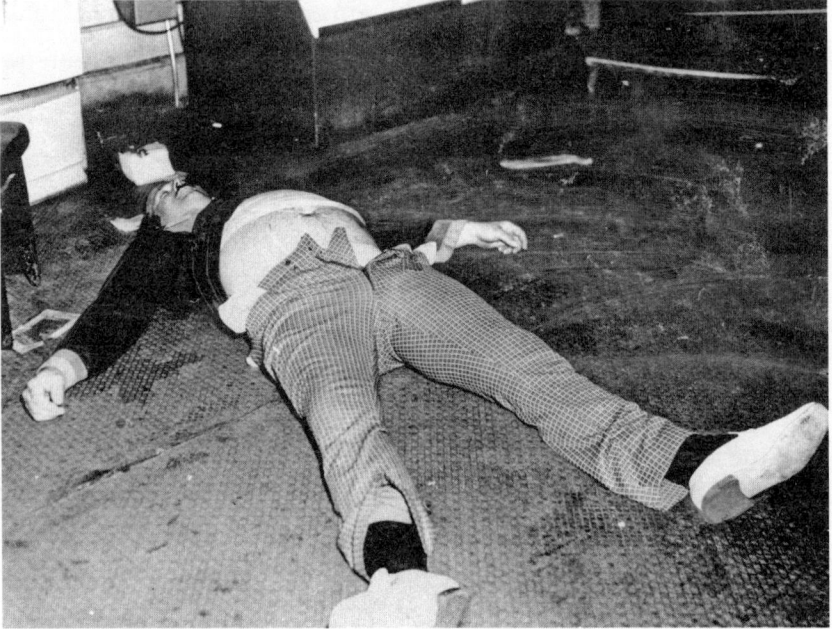

The body of James 'Jimmy' McBratney on the barroom floor of Snoope's on Staten Island, after being shot dead on 22 May 1973 by John Gotti and his accomplices, Angelo 'Quack Quack' Ruggiero and Ralph 'Ralphie Wigs' Galione.

The more I talked to Mike McGowan about how he went undercover in the American Mafia to help break their stranglehold on the cocaine trade in the US, the more I realized that this work was like an extreme form of method acting. He would have to 'cold infiltrate' Mafia groups, spending days, weeks, months in and around their known hangouts until he had earned their trust, and the opportunity to step inside the circle. As he put it, though, 'There's no take two.' If he had ever let his performance slip he would have been a dead man. Even then, there was every chance he could have ended up dead anyway – for example, as an innocent bystander gunned down in a violent spat between two rival factions. When you're spending all your time hanging around the Mafia, it's all too easy to be in the wrong place at the wrong time. And the consequences can be deadly.

Mike had lived to tell the tale. But something he said left no doubt in my mind of the risks he and his colleagues had taken back then – and of the impact that work would always have on their lives. 'This is the first time I've ever sat in a bar with my back to the door.' Those words reminded me that to work undercover, especially infiltrating a group as powerful and deadly as the Mafia, meant a life of looking over your shoulder.

While Mike's undercover operations predominantly targeted lower-level operatives, they also were part of a wider intelligence- and evidence-gathering drive that US attorney Rudolph Giuliani was about to combine with one of the most powerful laws at his disposal in a bid to take down New York's Five Families. While it had become law on 15 October 1970, the Racketeer Influenced and

Corrupt Organizations Act (RICO) only truly became a game changer in terms of targeting organized crime when it was aggressively implemented in pursuit of the US Mob in the 1980s. RICO's purpose was 'the elimination of the infiltration of organized crime and racketeering into legitimate organizations operating in interstate commerce', so it required the crimes to cross state lines. To be able to prosecute using RICO, the authorities also needed to show that two or more separate instances of racketeering had occurred within ten years of each other. And while RICO cases carried a maximum sentence of 20 years in prison, that could be less than some of the other more serious crimes the accused might also be suspected of – such as murder. However, the law did allow the government to seize all profits pertaining to RICO crimes – and for any injured parties to sue for triple the damages caused. But the single biggest benefit of the law was that by pursuing a RICO case the authorities could finally prosecute the top dogs in criminal organizations based on evidence gathered from their rank and file. US Mob bosses could be taken down – sentenced for up to 20 years and with their money seized – so long as the prosecution could gather enough evidence to show their organization was committing these crimes. The dons could no longer claim 'plausible deniability' – saying 'I didn't know nothin'' was no defence.

The man who became the poster boy for America's war on the Mob, the figurehead who brandished the sword of RICO, was Rudolph William Louis Giuliani. 'Rudy' was born in an Italian-American neighbourhood of Brooklyn, New York, on 28 May 1944. His paternal grandparents were originally from Tuscany.

His father was a convicted criminal who had served time at the infamous Sing Sing prison and who afterwards worked for his brother-in-law as an enforcer for his loan sharking and gambling operation. Despite this, Rudy graduated high school then college and, having put aside his earlier inclination to become a priest, enrolled in the New York University School of Law in Manhattan – and graduated *cum laude*. He gained a reputation for his tigerish cross-examinations as he worked his way up the legal ladder – and in 1981 he was appointed associate attorney general, the third highest position in the Department of Justice, in the administration of the new president, Ronald Reagan.

In 1983 Giuliani took up the post of US Attorney for the Southern District of New York. While ostensibly a demotion, this was actually an appointment that Giuliani had sought – as he had a burning desire to prosecute, and litigate, high-profile cases including those against the New York Mob. It was also a position from which many before him had launched political careers – it was known as a springboard to running for public office.

It did not take long for DA Giuliani to go to war with the Mob. He knew his biggest chance of nailing the Mafia in his city was to build a bulletproof RICO case against the Five Families using the intelligence and resources of the Federal Bureau of Investigations. But bringing a RICO case, especially against one of the biggest, richest, most powerful and most deadly organizations in the history of organized crime, required a huge amount of work – and carried a huge amount of risk. And it was people like Mike and his colleagues at the FBI who were on the front line.

Mike knew that the life-threatening work he was doing 'finding shit out' could help topple organized crime in America. All those months gaining the trust of mobsters, the weddings, funerals and christenings, had a very real end goal. For him, the work – in the lion's den with real-life wise guys – was a rush, a high that very few people will ever get to experience. But it was also the ultimate act of betrayal.

'You gain their trust, you get them to tell you things they shouldn't tell anybody. . . and then you betray them. And if you can't do that, you shouldn't be an undercover agent. And I've never betrayed anybody who didn't commit a serious crime.'

I couldn't help but wonder if, having insinuated himself into the lives of not just these men but also their wives and children, only to betray their confidence and their trust in him, he had ever felt a pang of guilt or remorse for his numerous deceptions. His response left me in no doubt. 'No. Never.' I believed him. I can tell that that certainty is likely the only way you can do the kind of job Mike did, the only way you can sleep at night. Even if it is with one eye open.

In early 1985 New York DA Rudy Giuliani got his wish, as he brought a massive RICO case to trial. The Mafia Commission Trial ran for nearly two years – from 25 February 1985 to 19 November 1986. Giuliani's stated intention? 'To wipe out the five families.' It was dubbed the 'case of cases' by *Time* magazine, who claimed it was 'the most significant assault on the infrastructure of organized crime since the high command of the Chicago Mafia was swept away in 1943'.

Giuliani's case was built on evidence amassed by the FBI that revealed the structure of the US Mafia, the existence of The Commission, and the role of the Mob in controlling key labour unions and corruption centred on major construction projects across New York, as well as the waste haulage industry in Long Island. The 11 defendants – the highest ranking Mafia figures in America – faced charges including extortion, labour racketeering and even murder. All of the bosses of the Five Families were prosecuted – Paul 'Big Paul' Castellano of the Gambino crime family, Anthony 'Fat Tony' Salerno of the Genovese family, Anthony 'Tony Ducks' Corallo of the Lucchese family, Philip 'Rusty' Rastelli of the Bonanno family and Carmine 'Junior' Persico of the Colombo crime family.

On 16 December 1985, ten months into what would be a twenty-one month trial, 'Big Paul' Castellano was assassinated outside the Sparks Steak House – as John Gotti took his opportunity to take out his boss and rise to the top of the Gambino family. At just before 5:30pm, Castellano was gunned down by multiple shooters as he got out of his car outside the restaurant. The *coup de grâce* was delivered as a shot to the head. The driver, Thomas 'Tommy' Bilotti, was shot as he tried to escape from the vehicle. It had been the promotion of 'Tommy' to underboss by Castellano that had been one of the factors in pushing Gotti into offing his boss. Watching from a car across the street, John Gotti drove over to see Castellano's dead body before leaving the scene.

As a result, the Mafia Commission Trial did not ultimately prosecute a Gambino family boss. And, when it was discovered that the Bonanno family had been kicked out of The Commission in the early 1980s following their infiltration by FBI agent Joe Pistone posing undercover as Donnie Brasco, their boss, Rusty Rastelli, was removed from the trial. He was, however, later indicted on separate racketeering charges.

The Donnie Brasco affair is another fascinating story, and one made famous by the film directed by Mike Newell and starring Al Pacino as Benjamin 'Lefty' Ruggiero and Johnny Depp as real-life FBI agent Joseph D. Pistone. In the spring of 1976, Pistone had volunteered to go undercover to infiltrate the Bonanno crime family. With his Sicilian heritage and fluent Italian, he was the perfect man for the job. His identity was to be Donald 'Donnie' Brasco – a jewel thief. He even attended FBI gemology courses to ensure his cover story would stand up. His initial break was to become an associate in one of the other Five Families – as he teamed up with a Colombo family crew that specialized in hijackings and robberies. After six months earning trust, 'Donnie' managed to forge a friendship of sorts with Anthony 'Tony' Mirra – a moody, violent member of the Bonanno family. Tony introduced him to Lefty Ruggiero and soon the man they knew as Donnie was working on the Bonanno family's illegal slot machine business.

When Tony Mirra was sent to prison, Donnie started working directly for Lefty. Lefty was a Bonanno soldato, and he tutored Donnie in the ways of the US Mob. When Carmine Galante, the unofficial acting boss of the Bonanno family, was gunned down while eating lunch on the patio of a Brooklyn Italian-American restaurant – a contract hit approved by The Commission after he had made a power grab and tried to corner the drugs market for himself – Donnie began to report directly to caporegime Dominick 'Sonny Black' Napolitano. It was Sonny Black who decided to vouch for Donnie, and to help him to become a 'made man' – a full member of the US Mafia. He wanted to enlist Donnie's help in a hit on a rival member of the Bonanno family, which was busy tearing itself apart. Sonny Black contracted Brasco for the hit, but when the FBI got wind of the plan they pulled the plug on Pistone's operation. The undercover officer had been keen to go ahead – but to fake the assassination as a way to convince Sonny Black and his bosses that he had 'made his bones' (killed on behalf of the Mob) and could become a made man.

After Pistone was pulled out, it became clear that Napolitano had very nearly made an undercover FBI agent a made man. Not long after, Sonny Black was shot dead, his hands cut off. Within weeks, Lefty Ruggiero was arrested – he would end up with a 15-year sentence. A few months later, Tony Mirra was killed. Pistone received a $500 bonus at the conclusion of his operation. The US Mafia put a $500,000 bounty on his head, and kicked the Bonanno's out of The Commission.

By the time of the Mafia Commission Trial, The Commission had rescinded the hit on Pistone for fear of the reprisals for killing an FBI agent. But the man who had been heading The Commission and who had cancelled the hit, Paul Castellano, head of the Gambino family, was dead. And the Bonanno family was still on the outside. And so, on 19 November 1986, after nearly two years in court, and following six days of deliberation by the jury, the three remaining bosses of the US Mob's Five Families – Tony Ducks Corallo, Fat Tony Salerno and Junior Persico – were each convicted of racketeering. On 13 January 1987 Judge Richard Owen sentenced each of the leaders of the Lucchese, Genovese and Colombo families to 100 years in prison. All three were also fined $250,000.

Just four months later, Giuliani was able to strike another blow at the heart of the US Mafia, this time against the Bonanno family. And this time the target was the international heroin operation that would soon become famous as the Pizza Connection. In a 17-month trial that had begun during the Mafia Commission proceedings, Giuliani was able to prove links between pizza parlours owned by the Bonanno family and the importation, and sale and distribution, of heroin from the Cosa Nostra – Palermo's Sicilian Mafia. The case had been made thanks to a series of coordinated raids conducted on 9 April 1984 – as the FBI uncovered guns, ammunition and huge amounts of cash in homes and pizza parlours across the USA. In March 1987 the epic $50 million trial began of Salvatore 'Toto' Catalano, a boss of the Bonanno clan who was uncovered as one of the masterminds of the international drugs ring – he was sentenced to 45 years in a federal penitentiary and fined $1.15 million.

By the end of the 1980s the efforts of Mike and his FBI colleagues had gathered enough evidence to enable Giuliani to successfully prosecute entire wings of the American Mob. The only family that seemed to have been mostly spared up until this point were the

Gambinos. But, in the 1990s, Rudy would finally get his man. It was an open secret that John Gotti was the boss of the Gambino clan, and that he had been voted into power by his capos despite having orchestrated the murder of his predecessor, Big Paul Castellano. In March 1987 Gotti – not long after ascending to the top of the Gambino family – had been acquitted in his own racketeering trial, thanks to a compromised juror. It had been a big shock at the time, coming hot on the heels of the successful Mafia Commission and Pizza Connection trials – and it led to the media dubbing the charismatic Gotti 'The Teflon Don'. It seemed no matter how they tried, the DA's office, Rudy Giuliani and the FBI could not make a case stick against John Gotti. But eventually, following an extensive period of surveillance and investigation – and acting on a wealth of incriminating evidence gathered using listening devices planted in the Gambino's HQ at the Ravenite Social Club – the authorities were ready to make one last attempt to get Gotti. On 11 December 1990 FBI agents and NYPD detectives raided the club and arrested Gotti. He was charged with five murders, conspiracy to murder, loan sharking, illegal gambling, obstruction of justice, bribery and tax evasion. Then in late 1991 one of his co-accused, his newly appointed underboss Salvatore 'Sammy the Bull' Gravano, agreed to turn state's witness. Gravano was crucial in the trial – he had been one of the men who had shot Paul Castellano, he was one of Gotti's co-conspirators and he knew where the boss's bodies were buried, both literally and metaphorically.

On 2 April 1992, after a relatively swift 14 hours of deliberation, Gotti was found guilty on all charges by a jury of his peers.

James M. Fox, Assistant Director in Charge of the FBI's New York Field Office, announced at the subsequent press conference: 'The Teflon is gone. The don is covered with Velcro, and all the charges stuck.' On 23 June 1992, John Joseph Gotti was sentenced to life imprisonment without the possibility of parole and ordered to pay a $250,000 fine. He would never again know freedom. In 1998, while incarcerated, Gotti was diagnosed with throat cancer. He underwent surgery to remove the tumour at the United States Medical Center for Federal Prisoners in Springfield, Missouri. But two years later the cancer was back. Gotti returned to Springfield for further treatment, but in 2002 his condition began to rapidly deteriorate. John Joseph Gotti Jr. died on 10 June 2002. He was 61 years of age. An estimated 300 onlookers followed his funeral procession, which passed Gotti's Bergin Hunt and Fish Club on its way to the gravesite – but it's believed none of those present were senior members of the Five Families. By now it seemed the US Mob had decided Gotti's actions had tarnished their reputation.

At 12:17pm on 26 February 1993 a van exploded in the underground parking garage below the 110-storey North Tower of the World Trade Center. Fortunately the explosion caused by the 1,000lb bomb failed to cause the North Tower to collapse into the South Tower, but nonetheless six people, one of them a pregnant woman, died. Over 1,000 were injured, and 50,000 were evacuated. James M. Fox was the man tasked with the investigation, and with bringing the al Qaeda cell responsible, a group of seven led by Ramzi Yousef, to justice. Having led the investigation into the bombing, Fox – the man who helped put Gotti behind bars – retired from the FBI in 1994, just weeks before the first four suspects in the attack were found guilty. He had served the FBI for 31 years. But he died at Mount Sinai Hospital in New York in 1997, of complications from sepsis, aged just 59 and having only had three years to enjoy his retirement.

In the early 1990s Rudy Giuliani, the DA's office and the FBI were effectively combining, and securing long sentences, seizing assets and imposing significant financial penalties on all of the biggest players in the US Mafia. Even if the wise guys could hack being sent to jail, the federal authorities were able to take their homes, their cars, their businesses and their savings. It was crippling for the Mob. The tide was turning. As the convictions stuck, more and more mobsters were prepared to flip – to give evidence against those higher up the food chain. And with the courts empowered by the ability to hand down lengthier sentences than ever before for drug crimes, given to them by President Reagan, 30-year sentences became commonplace.

The first person I had met on my US trip, Salvatore 'Crazy Sal' Polisi, was one of those who faced the double whammy of RICO and lengthy sentences for drug crimes. Arrested on drug charges, he had faced years behind bars. He had cooperated and had given evidence against his former bosses. Anthony Ruggiano Jr. testified in six Mafia trials. Even Dominick Cicale, perhaps the coldest and hardest of all the criminals I had met so far, eventually got tired of the treachery of 'the life' and, facing a new murder trial, decided to cooperate with the government. In contrast, the friendly, silver-haired man I had met, George Martorano, had been sentenced to 32 years for drug offences – the longest custodial sentence ever handed down for a non-violent crime.

America's successful crackdown on the Mob had an unexpected effect, however. With the Mafia crippled, the full might of the US authorities and their war on drugs was let loose on the source of the cocaine that had made the American Mafia so rich and powerful: the Colombian cartels. But, with the Colombians now finding their North American distribution decimated by the hobbling of the US Mafia, would they have to find other markets, and other partners, for their product? One thing was certain: I had a new destination for my investigation. I was off to Colombia.

Before we left Miami for good, we had one last filming job, though – the regular attempt to get a drone up and record some aerial shots of the city. Having had our attempts in Philly thwarted by a gang of pigeons, and knowing that what the drone had revealed of Atlantic City was unlikely to ever see the light of day, I was somewhat apprehensive. Not least because in Miami any commercial drone filming requires the permission of the police – and the attendance of a police officer. But when our guy arrived my concerns were instantly allayed. He was like something straight out of central casting. Young, tanned and muscly, he was the archetypal Miami PD officer – immaculately dressed in his pressed and polished uniform. An enormous cigar in his hand, his eyes hidden behind mirrored aviator sunglasses, he smiled as he greeted us and before long he was offering to take us out on a police boat the following day. We never did take him up on his offer of a ride along in the police boat – but he ensured we were well looked after and this time our drone filming went off without a hitch. It was a relief to enjoy the lighter side of Miami and bask in the sun briefly, after what had been a very eye-opening few days. That night we had our last meal on the US leg of our trip. The following day we would be off to Colombia.

PART THREE

Chapter Eleven

A Colombian Cocaine Bust

———

The trail of breadcrumbs I had followed on my investigation had taken me from a London assassination to a meeting with a Mafia member in Italy and then on to encounter former made men from the US Mob in the States. The next leg of my epic journey to uncover the links between one of the world's oldest and deadliest organized crime groups, the Mafia, and Great Britain, took me 5,000 miles from the UK all the way to Colombia.

In 2023, as I made my trip, Colombia was the world's top coca cultivator, producer of 60 per cent of the planet's cocaine supply. The areas of the country planted with coca bushes had reached a record high. And it was Colombian cocaine that the US Mob had moved across the United States in the 1980s – distributing coke from both Pablo Escobar's Medellín Cartel out of Miami and from the Cali Cartel via their New York hub. In the '80s Colombia supplied around 80 per cent of all the cocaine in the USA. The cartels were making hundreds of millions of dollars a week from the trade. Billionaire drug kingpin Pablo Escobar made it onto the *Forbes* rich list in 1987 and was there for seven years straight until his death. Medellín, Colombia's second city and Pablo's home town, was the murder capital of the world. I was keen to find out how the relationship between the South American country's infamous drug cartels and the Italian Mafia might have led to the forging of a connection with the UK as part of the global cocaine trade.

I flew into the airport in Cali. Nestled in the Cauca Valley, this was one of the key cities associated with the Colombian drug cartels and the cocaine trade. Even today, as I arrived, I knew the UK government's official travel advice counselled against all but essential travel to large parts of the Valle del Cauca Department. It was here that the infamous Cali Cartel, run by brothers Gilberto and Miguel Roberto Rodríguez Orejuela, was based.

Gilberto was born in 1939, Miguel in 1943. Gilberto left school at 15 but having worked as a clerk at a pharmacy he rose to become the manager, and by the age of 25 he had opened his own pharmacy. But by then he was already involved in criminal activity, having started out in kidnapping before progressing into the drugs trade. In the early 1970s he and his brother, together with José Santacruz Londoño and Hélmer 'Pacho' Herrera, formed a loose collective of criminals in the Cali region that ultimately became known as the Cali Cartel. The brothers were the de facto leaders, and Gilberto, known as 'the Chess Player' for his long-sighted and strategic approach, was the brains of the operation. Miguel was the guy who ran the day-to-day operations.

As cocaine not only overtook cannabis but also heroin, and rose to become the most valuable drugs commodity of the 1980s, the Cali Cartel expanded and became partners with Pablo Escobar and his Medellín Cartel. But their wildly different personalities, and their diametrically opposed attitudes to the best ways to do business, and protect their power and vested interests, turned them from allies to deadly enemies. With Pablo waging what at times seemed like a one-man war against the Colombian government, the police, the justice system and the general population, the Cali Cartel plotted to assassinate their partner-turned-narcoterrorist. And, when their attempts failed, they assisted in the formation of the paramilitary kill squad known as *Los Pepes* (*Los Perseguidos por Pablo Escobar* – Those Persecuted by Pablo Escobar), which devoted itself to destroying Pablo and the Medellín Cartel.

However, the fall of Pablo and his cartel did not save his rivals, the brothers in Cali. Instead, the death of Pablo on 2 December 1993 – shot dead on a rooftop in Medellín during a gun battle with Colombian forces – merely served to train the spotlight on those who would seek to fill the void left by his passing. Soon the Cali Cartel, and the Rodríguez brothers in particular, were not just Colombia's but the USA's 'most wanted'. It was not long before they were arrested – and eventually both were extradited to America. Miguel, now in his 80s, is still in prison in the US, serving a 30-year sentence for his crimes; older brother Gilberto died in an American prison medical centre in 2022, aged 83. But even after the removal of the Rodríguez brothers, the Cauca Valley was still a hot bed of cocaine production. And I was about to find out just how true this was.

But first there would be a lot more of one of my least favourite things – waiting. We had been in regular communication with the

Colombian army to arrange to join them on an operation in the Cauca Valley. But this was proving to be more complicated than we had anticipated. The initial plan had been for us to travel to a small coastal town, right in the region that the UK's Foreign Commonwealth and Development Office (FCDO) advised against visiting. From there the Colombian army were going to fly into the jungle in helicopters and begin to clear the area, and we would follow them in our own chopper and join them on the clean-up before flying out again. But in the end the army were unable to get sign-off for the petrol required for the mission, and we were back to square one. Then they came to us with another plan. This time we would be going with the army out into the countryside around Cali, and not in helicopters but in a convoy of huge, armoured trucks. Just hours away from the start of this mission we got a call updating the plan once more. They had decided this needed to be a night mission. As a result they would be going ahead to recce the region that evening. My job was to report to their forward operations base at 9am the next morning for a day of briefings and training, before then going out that night to their main command post to join the mission in the dark.

Everything the Colombian army were telling us about this new plan made it sound like it was significantly more complicated, and more dangerous, than the two previous iterations of the mission. We now only had a few hours to clear these significant changes with the production team back in the UK and, crucially, with our health and safety advisers and insurance company. It was a mad scramble to come up with a new risk assessment plan that reflected the dangers we might now be facing, and to get that agreed in time for me to join the mission. But, thanks to the kit that we were carrying which included GPS trackers and satellite phones, we managed it. After days of frustrating delays and changes, we were finally good to go. The mission was on.

But the next day the plan began to slide. First we were asked to wait until the afternoon to arrive at the base. Then 2pm became 3pm. The day was slipping away. Eventually, as the sun set, I drove out into the hills beyond the city. I finally arrived at a squat, whitewashed compound, surrounded by watch towers, after night had fallen. The headlights of our SUV picked out the mural on the wall at the entrance that announced that this was the command post for the Apolo special operations unit of the Colombian army. I was there to join the Apolo team on a raid deep into the Cauca Valley, on the hunt for active cocaine laboratories. The mission? To locate and destroy these labs. I walked in out of the darkness, through the open hangar doors and into a brightly lit meeting room. Several serious-looking men, decked out in their army camouflage, were sitting around the central table layout. I immediately identified the leaders of the unit and greeted them. Once we had shaken hands it was straight down to business. Colonel Peña, the commander of Apolo operations, addressed the assembled men – speaking in English for my benefit. He highlighted the risks of that evening's mission, stressing that it was dangerous not just for us but also for civilians. But I was soon to find out that the local population were not just at risk – they might also be a threat to us.

We were to mount an operation inside territory that was loyal to the cartels. The local population were dependent on the income brought to the region by the cocaine trade. They would be more than prepared to defend themselves against any threat to the hidden processing plants – and their livelihoods.

As the briefing progressed, we were brought out little pots and spoons. Inside was a kind of rice pudding with little currants in it. It was a welcome snack, but it was certainly a surreal moment eating a pot of rice pudding while Colonel Peña took the senior members of the unit through the specific roles assigned to their teams, the colour-coded troop graphics displayed on the interactive whiteboard behind him. We were also given more details on some of the risks we would be facing out on the mission. We were made to understand, in no uncertain terms, that there would almost certainly be gunfire. Not only that, but there would be the very real risk of getting caught in crossfire – with bullets flying in from opposite directions, potentially from our own troops and any hostile combatants. It was an added layer of stress at the end of a long, frustrating day – and we hadn't even got to the hard, dangerous part yet. In particular I could see our cameraman, who had been by my side from day one of this investigation, steeling himself for what might lie ahead. I knew he had a pregnant wife back home and I wouldn't have blamed him if he had decided this operation in the Cauca Valley was a risk too far even for him. Luckily for me, and for the programme, he decided to come along.

Out in the compound's courtyard the men made their final preparations and, wearing the dark clothes the colonels had specified, I donned the heavy body armour. Heading into a potentially deadly situation, I was, not for the first time, grateful for the experience that I and my team had gained over years of filming on the front lines of conflicts. The men loaded up into SUVs, their dull black rifles on their laps or clasped in their hands, and I took my place alongside them – unarmed, but sporting the same battle helmet and goggles. The convoy drove off into the pitch black of the Colombian night.

I was struck by the fact that the senior leaders had only informed their men of the location of the night's mission a mere three or four minutes before we set off. Even in 2023 it was clear that the Colombian army had concerns that its members might be loyal to the traffickers, that they might inform the cartel that we were coming and torpedo the operation. The war on drugs here is clearly far from over, and Colombia is still a key component in the global drugs trade – the country provides over half the world's supply of cocaine, over a thousand metric tonnes a year.

After what felt like an eternity of winding, pothole-littered roads snaking up and up, we finally pulled to a halt. It was 1am and we were far from the lights of any town or village, in the foothills of the Andes Mountains. The men loaded their assault rifles, and we prepared to leave the road and head into the dense undergrowth on foot, and under cover of almost total darkness. When we left the vehicles we were already at 4,000 feet. We were urged to stick close together, the minimal light permitted for my cameraman occasionally picking out details – the grim set of a soldier's face; a pair of hands holding a rifle, one finger poised over the trigger guard; black army boots marching through the long grass. The mission became an endurance challenge, as we marched for hours on end through the dark, climbing an energy-sapping and lung-busting further 4,500 feet and all the time wearing the body armour and helmet that I was not allowed to remove. I could feel a nervous energy transmitted among the men, the sensation not unlike that which I've experienced in other, similarly dangerous situations in active war zones such as Afghanistan, Iraq and Syria.

As we marched further, our lights picked out row upon row of low green bushes – coca leaf. These hills were full of coca. We were deep inside a key growing area for a Colombian drugs cartel, surrounded by the plant that gave them wealth and power. I knew that the process for making cocaine from these leaves was relatively basic, that the technique had hardly changed for decades.

Colombia's economy had been built on coffee, the high altitudes afforded by the numerous slopes of the Andes mountains creating the perfect conditions to grow the arabica variety of coffee – the finest beans, in comparison with the less refined robusta type. But this crop, vital to Colombia's exports, had seen its value plummet and the industry had been decimated, in part due to a major global economic downturn. The regions where coffee had been their lifeblood, and their lifeline, needed a new and economically viable crop – and the thing that had made them so perfect for coffee production, their altitude, now became a major barrier to growing anything viable. One plant came to their rescue. The coca plant grows under very similar conditions to the coffee plant. And, unlike almost any other crop they could have cultivated at such altitudes, its value was sufficiently high that it was actually worth picking, growing and transporting. Coca had supplanted coffee, and the evidence was right before my eyes, planted in row upon row. And an additional advantage was that it was simple and cheap to convert the coca into cocaine right here – out in the wilderness of rural Colombia, among the crop itself. The technique has hardly changed over the decades. In basic and easy-to-disguise cocaine laboratories, laid out on sheets, the leaves would be chopped up before having salt poured over them. The salt would draw out the moisture released from the chopped coca leaves, creating a black, tar-like liquid. Deposited into barrels, the sticky leaves would have petrol poured over them before being covered and left overnight. The paraffins in the petrol would act as a solvent, further drawing out the 'coca base'. Next chalk would be added, the mixture put into a net and then squeezed out. This coca base would then be pressed into brick moulds where it would dry out, leaving a hard 'brick' of cocaine. It was the rudimentary but cleverly hidden cocaine labs where this process was carried out that we were hunting right now, in the pitch-black Colombian night.

I stopped for a moment, and explained on camera the potential dangers we were facing. Dangers that the camera operator behind the lens was more than aware of. I had been told that, if our presence was detected, the locals loyal to the cartel would surround us, kidnap us and take us hostage.

Life in large swathes of rural Colombia had been dangerous for decades. Out of the widespread political and social unrest and violence that raged across the countryside between 1948 and 1958, and became known as *La Violencia*, grew several powerful armed groups – principal among them the *Fuerzas Armadas Revolucionarias de Colombia – Ejército del Pueblo*, the Revolutionary Armed Forces of Colombia – People's Army, known as the FARC. This left-wing guerrilla group was at war with the Colombian state from 1964 until a ceasefire was agreed in 2016. But the long history of paramilitary and guerrilla activity on both sides of the political spectrum in Colombia, combined with the influence of the narcos, had cast a long shadow, and many of the tactics pioneered and exploited by both sides remained in use in the further-flung corners of the country. Co-opting the local citizenry, and armed kidnapping, were two such tactics that I knew were still common practice out here among the coca.

The word came down the column from up ahead, and I signalled with my hand to my cameraman. 'Kill it. Kill it.' We needed to turn off our light, and wait. I could hear a dog barking, and in the distance I could just about make out some lights. The soldiers thought they had finally located a lab. With a helicopter circling overhead, and the potential lab along the track up ahead, there was only one option – to press on. The soldier nearest to me announced that the team would strike at two points, and then – with the phrase 'green light' – the operation was on.

But as we descended into the hollow containing a cluster of buildings I could immediately tell that something wasn't right. A flashing neon sign lit up what looked like a man slumped on a chair against the brick wall below a peeling yellow poster that read merely '*tienda*' (shop). But it was a basic dummy, dressed in simple clothes, with a hat perched on its round head made from a volleyball that reminded me of Wilson from the Tom Hanks film *Castaway*. The soldiers searched the area, but there was nobody there, and no cocaine to be found. What they had discovered was one lab that had recently been dismantled and another that was in the process of being built. But the cartel must have known we were coming, as the lab under construction had been stripped and abandoned before our arrival. Bar the odd generator hidden beneath a hollowed-out plastic vat, there was next to nothing of any value left. The soldiers would decommission the site, but we all knew it would only be a matter of time before it was rebuilt, here or elsewhere. Taking down these cocaine labs must have felt like fighting the Hydra – for every head you chopped off, two more sprung up in its place. I didn't envy the men of the Apolo unit their task. Colonel Peña seemed to agree, when he told me that even when his sons have become grandfathers this problem will still be continuing in Colombia. It was a never-ending battle.

I had asked the colonels if they had ever encountered any traffickers who had sent cocaine to the United Kingdom. One of them, not Peña but his colleague, had told me that just four months earlier they had seized one and a half tonnes of cocaine hydrochloride in the region, and that the six people involved were planning to export that product to Europe. Colonel Peña said what I was thinking – that it was Mafia groups who were the big problem. Where once it would have been the US Mob, now it was clear that it was the European-based organized crime groups, foremost among them the Italian Mafia, who were the new partners of the

Colombian cartels – and potentially responsible for the expansion of the cocaine trade into Europe, and Britain. To find out more, I knew I had to get closer to the cartels.

But before I had the chance, I had my first experience of Colombia's infamous FARC. We were on the road, driving back from the Apolo command post, when the driver of my SUV started to slow down. Craning my neck I could see a line of cars ahead, and beyond them what looked like some kind of hastily constructed checkpoint or roadblock. The driver said just one word to me: 'FARC.' The FARC might have officially laid down arms in 2016, but I knew that they had split into two factions – one had reinvented themselves as a legal political party, while a small group of dissidents had gone back on the peace deal and taken up arms once again. It was only as we inched closer that I was able to see the makeshift signs, posters and flags, and the plastic buckets, that revealed this to be a collection point for the legal, political wing of the modern-day FARC. It was effectively an illegal toll, dressed up as the chance to make a voluntary donation to their cause. But I wasn't having any of it – a three-hour operation that turned into seven hours, a toe that had turned septic, soaking wet – I was a grumpy Kemp and wasn't prepared to donate anything to anyone. I think the look in my eyes told him this wasn't a cause worth pursuing and we drove off. I have rarely been so grateful for my bed as when I was finally able to lie down in my hotel back in downtown Cali that night.

Chapter Twelve

The Cali Cartel and The US Mob

――――

Fresh from my long and ultimately fruitless trek through the foothills of the Andes, I was back in Colombia's capital Bogotá, a busy, bustling, modern city of some seven million inhabitants. And I was glad to at least be driving, and in daylight, to meet with someone who I hoped might be able to shed more light on the relationship between the Colombian cartels, the Mafia and the UK.

My destination was a sunny terrace, with a lovely view of the city of Bogotá beyond, and the man I had come to meet was US journalist and author Ron Chepesiuk. He has studied Colombia's cocaine trade since the 1980s, and mapped the growing global influence of the various cartels. As he told me, Pablo Escobar and the Medellín Cartel were the 'Henry Fords' of the international cocaine trade – they developed the transportation system that enabled the mass distribution of the drug into America. In contrast, he compared the Cali Cartel to McDonald's, as they were the group that developed this illegal business into a fully-fledged corporate enterprise. Although Pablo Escobar and the Medellín Cartel might have been better known around the world due to the bloody war they had waged on the Colombian government, in Ron's eyes the Cali Cartel were the most important drug organization that ever was.

Led by Gilberto Rodríguez Orejuela, the Cali Cartel tended to favour finding a pragmatic business solution to any problem over a criminal one – in stark contrast to the violence of Pablo Escobar and the Medellín Cartel. As I'd already discovered, initially this pragmatism brought them into an alliance with Pablo and Medellín – as they agreed to share the riches on offer in the United States and carve up the key territories between them. While Pablo would control Miami, the Rodríguez brothers would have New York. The Big Apple already had a significant Colombian population and, as I knew, it was also the home of the Italian-American Mafia – The Mob. The Cali Cartel couldn't distribute cocaine in New York without paying their dues to the US Mafia. Ron was sure that the Five Families, who knew everything that was going on in their city, would have not only been aware of the Cali Cartel but would most likely have worked out a deal and gone into business with them. After all, there were millions, if not billions, of dollars to be made. The New York Mafia and the Cali Cartel formed an informal alliance over the distribution of Colombian cocaine across the East Coast. Cali supplied the product, and the Mob ran the distribution.

But, as I had learned, the American authorities had gone after the Mob with significant success. And with their US Mafia partners on the ropes, and the Colombian cartels the next on the federal hit list, Cali had been forced to look for other significant markets for their lucrative product. Ever the shrewd businessmen, the Rodríguez brothers realized they could turn this setback into a major opportunity. As Ron told me, they expanded their operation to ship drugs right across Latin America, as well as into Europe, and were even considering opening up new markets as far afield as Japan.

I cut to the chase, and asked Ron if the Cali Cartel and the Rodríguez brothers had started to import their cocaine directly into the UK. Ron was convinced that Britain would have been an obvious choice – a large population of over 60 million, and the perception that it would be an easy target, with lax laws. But when I asked him if he knew what route they might have taken to get their product to market in the UK, he drew a blank. In his words, 'That's one of the best kept secrets in the history of the drugs trade.'

I was more convinced than ever that the Cali Cartel, with their entrepreneurial attitude and international approach to their business, were best placed to turn their attentions from America and instead seek to gain a stranglehold on the cocaine business in Europe. And that this 'cocaine corporation' had found a way to get huge quantities of their cocaine into the UK itself. The way they had managed to do this was still shrouded in secrecy, but I had managed to secure a meeting with someone who might just hold the key to unlock this mystery. Someone with intimate first-hand knowledge of the Cali Cartel. I was off to meet with none other than Fernando Rodríguez Mondragon, the son of Gilberto – the man who had established the biggest drugs cartel the world had ever seen.

In the mountains between Cali and Buenaventura, after an hour's journey, I drove the compact SUV hire car along an overgrown paved road. Ahead of me a solid but weathered and rusty-looking gate was opened by a security guard. The security camera housings on the guard house stared out vacantly. I was driving into the sprawling hillside complex that had been Gilberto Rodríguez's Cali home. This hacienda, like so many others belonging to the country's former cartel leaders, was now the property of the Colombian government.

As a family member of an outlawed cartel, Fernando had needed to secure special permission from the authorities to return to his father's property and show me around. Thankfully, he was waiting on the hacienda's porch to greet me. Not unlike his father and uncle, Fernando looked more like a regular working Colombian – perhaps a lawyer or an accountant – than anyone associated in any way with one of the biggest criminal organizations of the 20th century. Slight of stature and wearing glasses, he was casually dressed in a pink, short-sleeved shirt and jeans, and welcomed me with a friendly pat on the back (though the drivers were careful to refer to him as Don Rodríguez!)

We explored the hacienda together. It was the first time a film crew had ever been allowed inside, and it was like a building that had been abandoned in a hurry. I saw an overgrown basketball court and, down below the main house, a structure where Gilberto must have stabled his horses along with accommodation for 30 hitmen – I couldn't help thinking that however luxurious this was it must have been a bit like being in a prison you had built for yourself. When Fernando went ahead and I followed him, ducking through a low doorway, I could barely believe what greeted me: a four-lane ten-pin bowling alley, complete with its original automated ball-return machinery. In the far corner of the alley was a bar area, and beyond that a 'disco'. I marvelled at what all of this must have cost but, as Fernando pointed out, the point was not the money but just to show that you could – that you had the ability to build a bowling alley in the Colombian mountains. This was Gilberto's home, and he wanted to entertain his friends, family and associates here. And, to that end, absolutely nothing was impossible.

As we circled the hacienda's swimming pool, I asked Fernando if he knew how many houses his father had owned. His best guess was around 4,000 properties. I was curious how Fernando felt being back here in the family's home, where he no doubt had spent many a happy day diving into this now abandoned pool. His response was a philosophical one: 'My father died. I forgive him for every bad thing he did in his life. Hopefully God will take him to a better place than here.'

Sitting on the terrace of the former hacienda of Gilberto Rodríguez Orejuela, admiring the property's stunning view with the son of the former boss of the Cali Cartel, it all felt a long way from Blackfriars, from the murder of Roberto Calvi, and from the start of my long investigation into the links between the Mafia and the UK. But Fernando was about to help me uncover a vital piece of the puzzle, and join the dots between the Cali Cartel, the Italian Mafia and Great Britain.

I'd already discovered that 'the Chess Player' had begun to shift the focus of the cartel's cocaine distribution away from the US and towards Europe long before his arrest in 1995. But where had he shipped his cocaine to, how had he done it, and who had been his partners? Fernando began by filling me in on the origins of his father's cocaine smuggling route into America. In the mid-1970s the Cali Cartel had started off refining coca paste into cocaine powder in Colombia, then sending the coke into the US in suitcases. Soon they upgraded from a couple of suitcases to using planes – and filling them with up to 500 kilograms of cocaine at a time. Back then, a kilo of Colombian cocaine could be produced or purchased in Colombia for $1,700 – but in the States it was worth an eye-watering $60,000. Doing the maths, I quickly realized just how lucrative this was. Just one plane load could potentially net the cartel $30 million. It was no wonder the Cali Cartel got so rich, and so powerful, so fast. According to Fernando it only took four years for his father to become a billionaire. Soon the Rodríguez brothers were sitting atop a business with annual profits of up to $10 billion.

I already knew from my time stateside that in the late 1970s, when all this was going on, the American Mob, principally the Five Families, had immense power in New York. So it made perfect sense when Fernando explained to me that it was the Mob who provided the protection and distribution for his father's cocaine in the Big Apple and beyond. Fernando went one further, however – telling me that not only were the Cali Cartel and the US Mob business partners, they were even friends. He told me that John Gotti, who he referred to as John Joseph, the head of the Gambino family, not only spoke regularly to his father but that they even had several dinners together.

But the rise and rise of the Cali Cartel did not go unnoticed by their volatile ally, Pablo Escobar. Although he had agreed with the Rodríguez brothers to divide and conquer – that Medellín would have Miami and Cali could take New York – and even though he was making millions a day from his cocaine route into Florida, Pablo was more than a little jealous of the cash his rivals were banking further north and the prices they could command for their product in the Big Apple. As he sat opposite me, on the terrace of his father's former home, Fernando told me that all the troubles between the Medellín and Cali cartels stemmed from Pablo's attempts to muscle in on the lucrative New York market. Pablo knew the price of cocaine in New York was significantly higher than in Miami – something convicted killer and takedown merchant Dominick Cicale had confirmed when I met him in Florida. And so the Medellín Cartel had started sending some of their merchandise up to New York, in breach of their agreement with Cali. Although known for his generally diplomatic approach, Fernando's father knew this was no time to show weakness to his biggest rival. He began to kill anyone Pablo sent to New York. When Fernando said 'Pablo didn't like that', knowing what Pablo Escobar was like, I could well imagine what the possible repercussions would have been.

But it's hard to believe that in 1984 anyone in Colombia, let alone in the US or UK, could have imagined quite what Pablo Escobar would do to Colombia. . .

Pablo had risen from a youth of petty crime to become the violent and fearsome leader of the Medellín Cartel. But he had also dreamed of legitimacy. He believed that he could one day be the President of Colombia, and he had significant early success in his political career – even becoming elected to be a *suplente*, a stand-in, in the country's House of Representatives. But when the source of his wealth and influence was questioned, when he was called out as a brutal 'narco' dealing in cocaine and death, and when he saw his political dreams and aspirations crumble before his very eyes, he went to war with the state, setting off bombs and then assassinating the country's Minister of Justice, Rodrigo Lara Bonilla – the man who had publicly branded him a criminal and unfit for political office. Pablo Escobar had become the world's first narcoterrorist. As the Colombian police and armed forces responded, Gilberto decided he needed to get out of the country. And what Fernando told me next got my attention. His father had flown to London.

But, as a Brit who has travelled widely, what Fernando related next was a familiar tale. His father hadn't liked the food, he hadn't been a fan of fish and chips, and so when a friend offered him the opportunity to stay with him in Spain he jumped at the chance. That friend, it seems, was Jorge Luis Ochoa Vásquez – a fellow Colombian and one of the founding members of the Medellín Cartel. Jorge Ochoa had been one of the central members of the cartel from the start, alongside his brothers Juan David and Fabio, Pablo Escobar and his cousin Gustavo Gaviria, Carlos Lehder and José Gonzalo Rodríguez Gacha – known as

'El Mexicano' ('The Mexican'). The Ochoa brothers, originally from a family of cattle ranchers and restaurant-owners, had been closely allied to Pablo and his gang from the moment they collaborated against the M-19 guerrillas who had taken their sister Martha Nieves Ochoa Vásquez hostage in 1981. Jorge Ochoa stood six feet tall and weighed over sixteen stone, and loved bull fighting and Harley-Davidson motorbikes. He was also crucial to the Medellín Cartel's cocaine pipeline, overseeing the importation of the drug into America via Panama. And in the early 1980s Pablo's Medellín cartel and Gilberto's Cali Cartel were still very much partners in Colombia's global cocaine business.

It is believed that Gilberto may not only have been in Spain to enjoy the food and wine of the region with Jorge Ochoa, but might also have been looking to form strategic alliances in the country, not only with local Galician traffickers but even with the Camorra itself. But whatever the reason for his trip, his association with his fellow Colombian would cost him dearly when the man from Medellín made a schoolboy error. One night in mid-November, Ochoa went with his wife to one of the most famous restaurants in Spain, and drank numerous bottles of the establishment's most expensive Dom Pérignon champagne. Drunk, when he received their huge final bill of nearly 90 million Spanish pesetas, Ochoa paid in cash. That kind of behaviour did not go unnoticed. The restaurant owner called the authorities about the diners, and the police began looking into the man who was calling himself Moisés Moreno Miranda. They discovered that he had purchased an 800 square metre property, on a 10,000 square metre plot, that boasted a tennis court, swimming pool, nightclub and wine cellar. He was also hoping to acquire a 4,000 hectare farm in Andalusia.The Spanish police were convinced this man Moreno was actually Ochoa, a Colombian cartel member that Interpol had advised them that the DEA was requesting they track down in Spain – where they also suspected Gilberto Rodríguez Orejuela was hiding out – and they mounted a surveillance operation.

Close monitoring of Ochoa and his wife revealed regular meetings with another wealthy couple who were staying in a luxurious Madrid hotel. The man was supposedly Gilberto González Linares, a Venezuelan national, but the police quickly identified these new suspects as none other than Gilberto Rodríguez Orejuela and his wife Gladys-Miryam Ramírez. Gilberto had bought two large apartments in Madrid – both in his wife's name. At 9:30pm on 15 November 1984, the two couples were arrested as they left a rendezvous at their regular meeting place, an apartment on General Oraá Street.

Gilberto had opened a bank account in his wife's name and deposited a large amount of cash, as well as purchasing several Mercedes-Benz cars. When apprehended he also had on his person an accounting book, which the authorities believed was a ledger recording the sale of over 4,000 kilograms of cocaine in 1983 alone. Gilberto was convicted of money laundering and sent to Madrid's Carabanchel prison, the biggest prison in Europe, built during the time of General Franco. His wife was not convicted. Ochoa's drunken dinner had been an expensive one for the leader of the Cali Cartel, in more ways than one.

But, in a move more typical of his 'Chess Player' nickname, he turned his time behind bars to his advantage. Rubbing shoulders with some of Spain's most hardened criminals, Gilberto discussed ways they could work together to expand the Cali Cartel's cocaine operation into Europe. Gilberto saw huge benefits to exploiting this large, untapped market – not least the fact that it was beyond the reach of the machinery of American law enforcement that was so aggressively dismantling the network he had built with the help of the US Mob. However, if he wanted to concentrate on expanding his business, and diversifying his distribution, Gilberto would have to first take care of the rapidly escalating situation back home.

After two years behind bars in Madrid, Gilberto Rodríguez was eventually extradited back to Colombia rather than to the USA. At the same time Jorge Ochoa was also sent back to his homeland by the Spanish courts. In Colombia, and with America demanding his extradition on charges of conspiracy to import cocaine, Ochoa received a suspended sentence for the crime of falsifying documents relating to the importation of fighting bulls from Spain and promptly vanished. When he was finally tracked down and held in prison once more with the possibility of extradition to the States looming, threats made by 'The Extraditables' – a violent group that was the mouthpiece of Pablo Escobar and his cartel comrades – led to his release. Ochoa surrendered to the Colombian authorities of his own volition in 1991, during a period when senior cartel members were offered immunity from extradition and reduced sentences in return for handing themselves in – a route also famously taken by Pablo Escobar himself when he entered the prison he built for himself, La Catedral.

Back home in Colombia, Gilberto Rodríguez successful fought not only to overturn his conviction on drug charges but also his potential extradition to the United States. As a result, he was eventually released. Once he had gained his freedom, he began to hatch a plan that he hoped would resolve the chaos and bloodshed caused by the war, and the man behind it, instigator-in-chief Pablo Escobar, that was threatening his business.

I was told some more about Gilberto by his son Fernando later that day, when we moved down the mountain to film with him on the streets of Cali. One of the things I'd learned about Fernando was that he was very much known and respected in the local community, even though he was no part of his late father's cartel. In fact, he traded in collagen derived from sharks. It was a controversial practice, but it didn't seem like anyone down here was too bothered – they just knew who he was and I could tell this soft-spoken and intelligent man was not to be trifled with.

Fernando took me to the site of his father's very first pharmacy, the beginning of his legitimate business empire – the chain of local pharmacies that Pablo Escobar and the Medellín Cartel would later target in a brutal bombing campaign. But before Pablo, this first pharmacy would be destroyed by none other than Gilberto himself. Fernando told me how his father had blown up his fledgling business – in order to claim the insurance money. This cash windfall, when it eventually came, was the seed capital that he and his brother Miguel used to finance the start of their cocaine empire.

It was right here, where we were standing, that this combination of arson and insurance fraud facilitated the creation of what would become the Cali Cartel.

These sequences, shot on the streets of Cali were, not unlike in Philly, more than a little bit tricky. First of all this part of the city was dangerous. Our obviously foreign appearance, and the camera kit we were carrying around, quickly drew a lot of unwanted attention. Even with Fernando and our fantastic local 'fixer' there to help translate and smooth over any potential confrontations, the situation on the street threatened to turn a little ugly on more than one occasion – particularly when we went to the area where Gilberto Rodríguez had burned down his first pharmacy to finance his first consignment of cocaine. I've had plenty of experience filming in public in sketchy locations, and you can always tell when the mood turns. This was just one of those occasions. Thankfully, by this point we'd got everything we needed in Cali, and the next day we were going to be heading off to Colombia's high-altitude capital Bogotá. We decided to call it a day.

Chapter Thirteen

Killing Pablo

———

During my conversations with Fernando he had told me that in 1989 his father Gilberto had decided to kill Pablo Escobar, the leader of the Medellín Cartel and his former ally and now rival. His father and his uncle Miguel had made a deal with a group of highly experience mercenaries – many of them British former military men. I had heard something about this previously – of how the former SAS soldier Peter McAleese was recruited by military fixer Dave Tomkins and tasked with putting together a team to kill the world's most infamous drug lord in his own home. And all at the behest of the Cali Cartel.

McAleese had grown up in Shettleston in Glasgow, next to Barlinnie prison – where he could see his father signal to him from the cell window during one of his many stints inside. He had joined the Parachute Regiment in 1960 and from there graduated to the Special Air Service, the SAS, Britain's elite unit, in 1962. He fought with the SAS in Aden and Borneo but then in the 1970s and 1980s, having left the British armed forces, he became a mercenary in Angola, before joining the Rhodesian SAS and the South African

Defence Force's 44 Para Brigade. Back in the UK, he had been in the Booth Hall pub in Hereford one day when his old friend from Angola Dave Tomkins, one of the infamous 'Dogs of War' from the African nation's bloody conflict, turned up and offered him a job – in Colombia. And it was to kill Pablo Escobar.

Peter has admitted he didn't know much about Pablo, or about Colombia – all he knew was Pablo was not a good guy. He wasn't wrong. Born in rural Antioquia in 1949, Pablo grew up as the son of a bankrupt cattle farmer turned farm labourer and a school teacher. He was only a boy when a group of armed peasant guerrillas, a band of *chusmeros* from Colombia's years of strife known as *La Violencia*, burned his town. Pablo and his brother Roberto were sent to Medellín. And it was Colombia's second city that would become his true home, and the seat of his power. Here he began a life of petty crime that led him into the middle of the country's contraband economy. Eventually he graduated from smuggling illegal cigarettes to cannabis and then to bringing coca over the border from Peru. The rest, as they say, is history. Pablo created the Medellín Cartel, a collective of local Antioquenian cocaine smugglers and criminals, with the man now dubbed '*El Patrón*', 'The Boss', at the head.

As I'd discovered, in the early 1980s he embarked on a political career alongside his gangsterism, but his ambitious dream of becoming Colombia's president was shattered when his criminal background was publicly exposed by Minister of Justice Rodrigo Lara. This marked the turning point for Pablo, as he turned his now incredible wealth and power on his new enemy – Colombia itself.

His war with the government, the police, the army and the judiciary was a horrific one. Not only did he have politicians including Lara and presidential candidate Carlos Galán assassinated, but he set off innumerable bombs across Medellín, Cali and Bogotá. He put a price on the head of every policeman, and hundreds died – gunned down by Pablo's baby-faced assassins, his *sicarios*, and those who wished to become them, for a cash reward. By the end of 1989 he had become the world's first 'narcoterrorist' – as in November he blew up a passenger airliner, Avianca flight 203, and killed over a hundred innocent people. His target, Galán's successor César Gaviria, was not aboard.

It was in 1989, at the zenith of Pablo's reign of terror, that Dave Tomkins made his fateful offer to Peter McAleese. And it wasn't just the government of Colombia that wanted to see the back of 'El Patrón', it seems the Cali Cartel had had enough of their former partner's actions too. . .

Peter and Dave flew to Colombia at the behest of Jorge Salcedo, the Cali Cartel's head of security, and met with some 'businessmen' – who Peter later came to realize were actually the bosses of the Cali Cartel, Gilberto and Miguel Rodríguez – who asked them if it was possible to kill Pablo Escobar. For a man of Peter's background and experience, there was only one answer. Yes.

According to Fernando the crew demanded $10 million for the job, and insisted on getting paid up front. Whether they got their wish or not I'm not entirely sure. Not only did Fernando seem to know a lot about this shady deal to assassinate Pablo, he even told me he had footage of the mercenaries he could show me. He turned on his tablet and, right there on the hacienda's patio, I was able to watch images of men in military fatigues firing weapons and then, even more surprisingly, footage of a location that looked eerily familiar.

'That's here, isn't it? That bridge is still here!' The mercenaries hired by Gilberto and Miguel Rodríguez to kill Pablo Escobar had trained for their secret mission on the grounds of the property where I was sitting.

McAleese had helped recruit his team of fellow ex-SAS members and members of other special forces regiments turned mercenaries, and had trained them in Colombia for 11 gruelling weeks – including at the hacienda belonging to Gilberto Rodríguez Orejuela. They would get up at 6am and begin and end every day with intensive physical training to get fully fit for the mission. They had practised firing the weapons they had requested, and eventually had supplied by their Colombian hosts – everything from rockets, plastic explosives and grenades to M16 and Interdynamics MKR assault rifles – training in firing as a group, coordinating their attacks, as well as in embarking and disembarking from helicopters. Only when the unit was finally ready did Peter tell them what the target was. When it was revealed that one of the Rodríguez brothers had offered an extra cash bonus for the head of Pablo Escobar the soldiers started to argue over who would be the one to bring back the grizzly trophy.

Then Peter and Dave had a scare – they were contacted by British journalist James Adams of the *Sunday Times*, who had got wind of the plot. They flew to Panama to speak to him in person, and convinced him to hold off on publishing his story in exchange for an exclusive interview with them after the event. But with the knowledge that their plans were in danger of leaking, the timeline for the attempt on Escobar had to be moved up.

The Cali Cartel redoubled their efforts and managed to get a spy inside Pablo's lavish 700-acre Hacienda Nápoles. Then, on 2 June 1989, the call finally came in on the radio to alert the kill team that Escobar was at home. Fernando told me that the unit's plan was to throw dynamite from their helicopters – disguised in police colours – and that they also had a .50 calibre machine gun to make sure of the job. I know the size of the rounds used by such a weapon: they are nearly six inches long. This was a brutal piece of kit. But the mainly British squad had not allowed for the dangerous, changeable weather in the region. Peter himself had never been to Colombia before embarking on this mission; the closest he had come was some time in Guyana. Although he had been able to fly over the Hacienda Nápoles four times in advance of the mission, taking surveillance photos and studying the layout, it was from a great height and without circling or stopping to avoid their presence alerting the local radar operators who were all on Pablo's payroll.

Even with their helicopters disguised, Peter soon realized that Pablo's intelligence network meant the unit would have to fly in low, under the radar, to avoid detection. They couldn't afford Escobar getting tipped off about their approach. The team got into the choppers and headed up towards the Hacienda Nápoles. As they flew over the peaceful, pretty city of Manizales, just over 100 miles south-west of their final destination, Peter had no doubts he and his men were ready.

It was a lovely sunny day, but then clouds began to build over the Andes. The pilot of Peter's helicopter was young and inexperienced, and the combination of bright sunshine and complex cloud formations over the mountainous peaks created an optical illusion. They flew into cloud, then clipped the top of a peak and the chopper flipped upside down. As it came crashing to earth, the helicopter's blades carved through the trees and then bored several metres into the earth below. The pilot had lost his leg, severed by one of the blades that had scythed through the cockpit and only missing Peter because he had taken off his seatbelt and turned to warn Dave and the two other members of the crew to prepare for a crash. When they saw the pilot's limb had been practically destroyed, and that he was facing a slow, painful but inevitable death, they gave him a dose of morphine.

But it wasn't just the pilot who was in a bad way. Peter realized he was badly injured too, suffering from broken ribs and the aggravation of old injuries. His men bandaged him up and left him on the mountainous ledge as the second helicopter flew over their position, unable to reach them due to the dense undergrowth. Dave and the two other survivors headed down the mountain and were helped by some locals who miraculously weren't on Pablo's payroll. They helped the trio to find an open field where they were finally able to rendezvous with the other chopper and get spirited away.

But even with the assassination attempt called off, the risk was not over. There was the very real danger that Pablo might have found out about the failed attempt on his life, and so Dave had to convince Gilberto to scramble his own men to quickly retrieve Peter before Pablo could find and capture him. For the best part of three, long, rainy days Peter survived on a tin of beans he had managed to recover from the crash site and some biscuits. Each day the one remaining helicopter would fly over the crash site to assure Peter that he hadn't been forgotten. But all the while Pablo had his own teams scouring the region for survivors of the crash. When Peter heard Spanish voices from the slopes below his position he feared the worst. He cocked his Interdynamics assault rifle and readied himself. But as he prepared to fire, he heard them call out a name he recognized, and realized this was a rescue party of local mountain men sent by the Cali Cartel. His rescuers cut down a tree and trimmed off the branches, then strapped him to it with ropes. Peter was lowered down a series of drops attached to this makeshift stretcher. It was a long overnight trek to extract him. He was finally collected by helicopter and flown to a hospital for a quick patch-up job and then on to Cali.

Reunited, Peter McAleese had claimed the survivors from the attempt were paid a small fee by the cartel, then retreated to Panama to lick their wounds and prepare for a second attempt on Pablo. But, as the situation in Colombia evolved, it became clear that a new strike on El Patrón was no longer feasible. Peter and his crew flew back home.

The failed assassination attempt on his rival was a bitter blow for Gilberto. Dave and Peter did, however, plan one more attack on behalf of the Cali Cartel: a bombing raid on La Catedral, the prison that Pablo had built for himself as a condition of his surrender. But when Dave travelled to buy a Vietnam-era fighter jet for the attempt, a call tipped him off that the individuals to whom he had just handed $25,000 were undercover US customs agents and the arranged meeting was a sting. He fled back to Britain before the agents could apprehend him. It was the last attempt Dave or any British mercenaries would make on Pablo's life on behalf of the Rodríguez brothers. In the end, the increasingly open war between the Cali and Medellín cartels would only cease more than four years after the ill-fated helicopter sortie, with the eventual death of Pablo Escobar.

However, while this historic moment – the shooting of Pablo on a rooftop in Medellín in December 1993 – is generally credited to the actions of the Colombian army, police and the specialist unit the Bloque de Búsqueda, also known as Search Bloc, and to some extent also the paramilitary group, Los Pepes, Fernando suggested to me that his father had had a significant role to play. He told me that Gilberto Rodríguez had supplied the Colombian police with the triangulation machine that had enabled them to track down Pablo by pinpointing his location using his phone calls. It was this technology that had eventually led the authorities right to Escobar.

On 2 December 1993, having been on the run for nearly 18 months since his escape from his La Catedral prison and just a day after his 44th birthday, Pablo's luck finally ran out. His location was tracked to a Medellín neighbourhood and when he was found by Colombian police a gunfight broke out. First his henchman known as 'El Limón' was shot dead and then, finally, Pablo himself died in a hail of bullets as he tried to escape across the tiled roof. El Patrón, the fearsome leader of the Medellín Cartel, was no more.

And so, in the end, Gilberto had got what he desired – the end of his rival and a chance to focus his cartel, with their near-monopoly on the Colombian cocaine trade, on expanding into Europe.

His need was even more pressing given the situation in the States – where his US Mafia partner, Gambino family crime boss John Gotti, was now behind bars. As I had already discovered, Gotti had been sentenced to life without parole in 1992, just a year before the death of Pablo in Medellín, having been convicted of five murders, conspiracy to commit murder, racketeering, obstruction of justice, tax evasion, illegal gambling, extortion and loan sharking. He may not have been found guilty of anything directly relating to drug dealing, or his business with the Cali Cartel, but one thing was for sure: these charges had finally stuck, and the man known as 'The Teflon Don' was unlikely to be a free man again.

Chapter Fourteen

The Mafia, Spain and Colombian Cocaine

———

Gilberto Rodríguez decided to utilize the European criminal connections he had gained from his time in prison in Madrid. Fernando told me that his father passed on his contacts to one of his Cali Cartel members, and they made contact with the Italian Mafia. Soon they were doing business. Fernando even suggested that his father offered the Mafia a special, discounted price on his merchandise, so keen was he to cement this relationship and create a new pipeline and exploit a new marketplace. Despite dropping his wholesale price, the profits he and his cartel could make were still huge. It was clear the Italian Mafia had helped the Cali Cartel expand into Europe. As I left Fernando and drove down the valley away from his father's abandoned, dilapidated hacienda and the ghosts that inhabited it, I was more certain than ever that this connection between Cali and Italy must have led to new links being forged between the Mafia and Britain. After all, I knew that while Prime Minister Margaret Thatcher might have attempted to address the UK's heroin problem in the 1980s, there was no doubt that in the 1990s towns and cities across Britain had seen an influx of South American cocaine. It was beginning to look very much like the Italian Mafia might have had a huge role to play in that.

I knew that I needed to try to uncover what Ron Chepesiuk had told me, back on his sunny terrace in Bogotá, was 'one of the best kept secrets in the history of the drugs trade': the Cali Cartel's trade route into Europe, and from there into the UK. It seemed clear the Italian Mafia were key to this puzzle. And I had one further interview lined up while I was still in Colombia that should offer some clues.

I pulled off the main road, driving through the open set of chain-link gates and into what appeared to be a kind of junk yard. Shipping containers acted as a wall, lining the space, while others stood one atop the other in the middle of the dusty, bare earth, blocking my view ahead. As I pulled forward in the SUV, I caught sight of a man standing alone in the distance beside the rusting hulks of a selection of disused trucks. This must be the guy. I drove up to him, calling out his name – 'Fory?' – through my open window. I got out of the car. 'Fory?' It was only when I tried again, and extended my hand in greeting that I got a broad smile and a handshake in return. This was indeed our man.

Fory was a former Cali Cartel drug trafficker. As we walked through the yard, I asked him how he got involved with the cartel. He told me he had been 32 years old when he had come to know a man who went by the name 'El Caminante' – 'The Wanderer'. The Wanderer worked for the Rodríguez family. Having earned The Wanderer's trust, Fory was eventually made responsible for dispatching cartel ships, sending boats to Central America and North America. And then he said what I had been hoping to hear: 'and then Europe opened up'. Fory had personally met both of the Rodríguez brothers, Don Gilberto and Don Miguel. He told me that they were supportive of their workers, and that they paid well and rewarded loyalty: $500,000 could be earned for every successful shipment. It all fitted with what I had heard about the professionalism of the almost corporate Cali Cartel, in contrast to the blood and thunder of Pablo Escobar and the operation based in Medellín.

I asked Fory when the Cali Cartel first began shipping their Colombian cocaine into Europe. He couldn't give me an exact date, but said it must have started from about 1990. I could tell I was getting somewhere. Fory had first-hand knowledge of the Cali Cartel and the Rodríguez brothers' operation, and was on the front line of their export drive into Europe. And he seemed happy to talk to me. I pressed him further. 'What ports would you send the drugs to, in Europe?' Again, his answers sounded more than plausible: ports on the Spanish west coast – to avoid detection, the cocaine would be exported in concrete posts (though why this was never questioned by border forces is slightly beyond me – as they can be made very cheaply anywhere in the world!). I knew of Gilberto's links with Spain, and the ports of the Spanish coast would be ideal landing points for boats travelling all the way from Colombia.

Fory had been so open I decided to keep going, and asked him if he had ever travelled to Europe himself. Perhaps he had been on the ground in Spain and might be able to help me find the next link in the chain? He replied that yes, he had been to Europe on cartel business. The Cali Cartel had helped him secure a Venezuelan passport and sent him to Portugal. I needed to know who he might have met in Europe, and when I asked him I struck gold. 'I met with a man named Lombardo.' That name sounded distinctly Italian, rather than Portuguese or Spanish. I sought confirmation. 'Was he Italian?' 'Italian. He belonged to the Italian Mafia.' Jackpot. I now had a first-hand account of how the Cali Cartel exported Colombian cocaine into Spain with the help of the Italian Mafia.

Fory told me that the Cali Cartel and the Italian Mafia split the profits from their business arrangement 50–50 and that both sides might have been making billions of dollars from this new trade route. He explained that the Mafia were fairly rewarded for the risks they had to take in getting the drugs off the dock and distributing it across Europe. I asked Fory if he had any idea how much of the cocaine that he had helped export to Europe might have ended up in the UK. This time he couldn't put his finger on an exact number. But although he was not able to pinpoint that detail, I could tell from his response that plenty of Cali's product must have made its way to Britain. And I now knew for sure that it could only have done so through the distribution network of their partners – the Italian Mafia.

Chapter Fifteen

The Hendon Cocaine King

———

Having got as much as I could out of Fory, we shook hands and I got back into my car. As I drove back towards central Bogotá, mulling over what I had learned and frustrated that I hadn't yet found that final link between the Cali Cartel and Italian Mafia's joint European cocaine operation and the flood of Colombian cocaine entering Britain in the 1990s, I got a call from Ron Chepesiuk. It was as if he had read my mind. He asked me to come back to visit him – he knew someone who could tell me exactly how the cocaine cartels had reached the UK. His call had come in the nick of time. I was on my way back to the hotel to pack – we were due to fly out of Bogotá's El Dorado airport at 11pm that very night.

Back at his Bogotá apartment, Ron told me how in November 2003, a Colombian migrant working as a bus driver and living in Hendon, North London, had been arrested for importing cocaine with a street value of over £1 billion. Overnight, the previously unheard-of Jesus Ruiz-Henao had become the biggest name in the history of the British drugs trade. His was the largest operation of its kind that British police had ever uncovered, the first £1 billion cartel they had ever dealt with.

Ron told me he not only knew where Ruiz-Henao was now – in a maximum-security prison just on the other side of Bogotá – but that he had found a way for me to have a video call with him. And so, I sat down next to Ron at a small table by the window in his apartment, he turned on his laptop, and we were just moments away from speaking to the man Ron believed had pioneered the route of Colombian cocaine into Britain. Was I finally about to find the missing piece of the jigsaw puzzle – how the drug got from the Cali Cartel and Italian Mafia's distribution hub in Spain to the shores of the UK?

Then, as can often happen when you're filming for a documentary series – especially abroad – the unexpected happened. Our long-suffering cameraman, who had been looking progressively paler throughout the long, hot day, suddenly put down his camera, mumbled something inaudible, and stumbled out through the glass doors onto the balcony beyond. I heard him retching, and then the unmistakable sounds of him being suddenly and violently sick. Ever the professional, he had found a bucket into which to vomit to keep poor Ron's patio pristine. It became clear that he was not in a good way. He half-fell onto the large swing chair and lay down, and when we checked on him he was slurring his words. He was incredibly weak and turning delirious. The crew immediately got on the phone to try to secure some medical assistance. As they worked on getting help to our location as quickly as possible, my executive producer stepped into the breach, picking up a camera for the first time in I'm not sure how many years and pointing the lens at the table and chairs, and Ron's laptop. The clock was ticking, and we knew I couldn't miss my chance to speak to Jesus.

As the video calling software's artificial dial tone rang out, I mused over the fact that the man I was about to speak to was probably the most important drug dealer in British history – and a vital part of my investigation. I was desperate to get as much as I could out of talking to him, and when the call finally connected and I could see the tanned face of the man the British tabloids had dubbed 'Mr Big' and the 'King of Cocaine', I wasted no time. 'Jesus, let's go! Nice to meet you, I'm Ross Kemp.' As he put on his glasses, and stared into his screen, I could see a flash of recognition on his face. Jesus had lived in Britain for well over a decade after arriving as an asylum-seeker in 1990. It was one of the more surreal moments in my investigation when this unassuming-looking Colombian man in his 60s, in a dark sweatshirt and clean shaven, but speaking to me from Bogotá's high-security La Picota prison and known to me as the biggest drug lord in UK criminal history, replied in his fluent but heavily accented English with, 'Hold on! Ross Kemp! I know you're Ross Kemp!'

Conscious that the authorities might shut down our chat at any moment, I dived straight in, asking him when he first got involved in cocaine. He told me that he started out selling cocaine when he was around 17 years old, in Colombia. He would go and buy cocaine up in the mountains, where it was cheaper, and then sell it in the main cities where he could double his money. But he soon found that his small operation was likely to struggle, given the existence of the big players in the Colombian cocaine market – the cartels of Cali and Medellín. In a bid to forge a path for his criminal enterprise, Jesus thought laterally – and looked to Europe. As he told me: 'I was looking to Europe, and especially into UK.' At the time the Medellín Cartel was focused on Miami, and the Cali Cartel on New York. America was a bigger prize, much closer geographically to Colombia, and with existing routes pioneered by Pablo Escobar and his associates and rivals. But Europe was still a relatively untapped market.

Jesus told me he had moved to the United Kingdom in 1985, although reports suggest it might actually have been 1990 when he claimed asylum. He told me how his operation had started out small, a far cry from the £1 billion empire he had built by the time of his arrest in 2003. Initially he was distributing his cocaine in the post, mailing big brown envelopes containing typically 250–300 grams at a time. But he was sending out his envelopes of coke nearly every day, and the mark-up he was able to make selling his product was astronomical. He told me he would make a 10,000 per cent profit selling his Colombian cocaine in the UK. As he said, 'Back then it was so easy.'

I was curious as to when, and how, he decided to move drugs in larger amounts. Jesus told me that after just two or three years 'they' – by which I would later come to learn he most likely meant him and his partner in the criminal enterprise, his brother-in-law Mario Tascon – decided they needed to up their scale. But they faced a problem. Not part of the Cali or Medellín cartels, Jesus's operation lacked the connections in the UK and beyond to be able to import and distribute a much higher volume. What they needed was a way to get the cocaine supply Jesus could source in his native Colombia into Britain safely – and at scale. They needed an 'in' at the ports.

Jesus told me that the first, crucial connection he made with the wider European organized crime underworld was with the Sicilian Mafia. I asked him where he had met with these Italian Mafia contacts – and his answer gave me the information I needed to finally close the circle: 'Russell Square area, Central London.' I pushed him to confirm that the Italians he met with in Central London, who would help him establish a route for his Colombian cocaine into the UK, were Italian Mafia. And confirm it he did. These Mafia operatives, based in the UK, told him they had good connections – and that they were very interested in helping him with his 'charlie', as he euphemistically called his cocaine.

Ron filled me in on why this opportunity would have appealed so greatly to the Mafia. At the time they were successfully importing and distributing a high volume of heroin into the UK – but this was a chance for them to break into the cocaine business in a big way. It seemed Jesus, a Colombian cocaine dealer in London, was the man who had helped the Italian Mafia expand into the British cocaine trade.

Jesus went on to tell me how this sea change in his importation network impacted his business. He was now receiving up to a tonne of his high-grade Colombian cocaine at a time. Not only that, he was able to sell an entire tonne in just a single day. These were staggering amounts. I could see now how Jesus was responsible for getting £1 billion worth of cocaine onto the streets of London in just ten years. He truly had been the 'King of Cocaine'.

As Jesus continued to explain how his 'cartel' had operated, it became clear that his cocaine was not typically arriving on container ships into British ports. What he told me was further confirmation of the cocaine pipeline I had learned so much about in Colombia. His cocaine had arrived in other European countries first, and then been moved on to the UK by lorry or light aircraft.

Indeed, in the raids that led to Jesus's capture, the authorities had seized 72 kilograms of cocaine hidden in pallets on board a lorry in Thurrock, Essex. The man who had run a charity called the London Colombian Appeal Fund, set up to help orphans and deprived children in his homeland, but was actually the UK's founding cocaine kingpin, was eventually sentenced to 19 years in an English prison, and it was recommended he should be deported back to Colombia immediately on his eventual release. This was how I had come to speak to him on a video call from his jail in Bogotá.

Knowing the clock was ticking on our conversation, I pressed Jesus to find out where in Europe his shipments had first made landfall. His answer? Spain. No sooner had he told me this than he was cut off. I'd lost him. But he'd given me vital information.

The key location for this new cocaine pipeline had become clear, and had to be the next stop on my global investigation into the links between the UK and the Mafia. I needed to get myself to Spain. But before then, we had a seriously sick crew member to tend to. The cameraman was fading fast. There was no way he'd be able to shoot the final part of my interview with Ron. We decided we needed to move him inside and let him lie down on a proper bed – but that meant re-setting outside for the final bits of filming. No sooner had we de-camped to the patio with Ron than we heard the unmistakable sound of drums. And I'm not talking a drumbeat on a distant stereo. We looked over the edge of the balcony only to be greeted by the unexpected, and at this point completely unwelcome, sight of a full marching band on parade on the street directly below us. There must have been 400 drummers, and the noise was incredible. At this point it just felt like this shoot was cursed. But we were fortunate to have a fantastic fixer working with us – something that is an absolute necessity when you're filming somewhere like Colombia. He headed straight downstairs and somehow managed to convince the band to hold off from their energetic and cacophonous performance until we'd finished recording. At the same time he was finally able to get hold of a local doctor, who promised us he'd be with us as soon as humanly possible.

I recorded my final questions with Ron as quickly as I could, and before you knew it the doc had arrived. He suspected food poisoning, but we were also sure that the incredible exertions our man had undertaken filming with me on the long, hot and unbelievably stressful shoot up in the coca fields with the Apolo team must have played a part. The bottom line was he was now dangerously dehydrated. It was scary how rapidly he had deteriorated. Fortunately, the local doctor had brought an intravenous drip kit with him – and I have no idea what was in the injection he gave him but the revival it inspired was something to behold. By the time we had packed up our kit and were ready to leave Ron and head to the airport, our cameraman was just about fit to fly.

Filming in Colombia had been an interesting experience, to say the least. It had been packed with highs and lows, action and incident – and had given me vital insight into the ways the cartels, the US Mob and even the Italian Mafia might have worked together. I'd met numerous brave and fascinating men, each with a story to tell. But I have to admit it was a huge relief to finally make it to the airport on time, and all in one piece, ready to return home and then head off on the next leg of my investigation.

PART FOUR

Chapter Sixteen

The Costa Del Crime

———

London, Preston, Aberdeen, Naples, New York, Philadelphia, Miami, Bogotá and Cali. I had already been on quite the journey, and racked up more than a few frequent flyer points, and miles in the hire car, investigating the links between Britain and the Mafia.

Having just about recovered from our Colombian expedition, next I flew to a part of the world well known to holidaymakers from across Europe: the south coast of Spain. But this was no sunshine break for me; I was on the trail of Colombian cocaine, trying to discover how the Italian Mafia smuggled shipments of the drug supplied by their partners the Cali Cartel into Britain in the 1990s.

The sun was shining, however, when I arrived at what felt like a lovely little holiday let to meet my first contact on the costa. I opened the electric gates and walked into a tidily tended garden complete with grass lawn and inviting swimming pool. But when I looked to the low, yellow-walled villa I was reminded why I was there. The man standing against the wall, hands in the pockets of his dark jeans, not only had the hood of his jumper pulled up over his head but was wearing a balaclava. His eyes stared straight ahead as I walked up to him. And yet, when he spoke, he seemed friendly – welcoming me in Italian and offering me a seat at the garden table. This was Francesco Mazzarella, a man I had been reliably informed was a former Mafia operative who had been active in Spain.

Perched on the garden furniture, he explained why he felt it necessary to wear a balaclava for our meeting. Just 18 months earlier there had been an attempt on his life in Naples. As a result, he would rather not reveal his face to me or our cameras. Francesco was part of the Neapolitan Mafia, the Camorra. As he spoke, his story reminded me of another former member of the Camorra, Gennaro Panzuto. Like Gennaro, Francesco told me he had grown up with violence from a young age. As a child he admitted he already went around carrying a lot of guns. He, like Panzuto, had a love for and fascination with weapons – and gained the nickname 'Francesco Hand Grenade' because he kept two grenades in his house. I was left in no doubt that Francesco was not a man to be messed with, especially when he told me he had been sent to prison for 'drug trafficking, weapons, extortion, robbery, theft, contempt. . . every conceivable crime'. This was a bad man. By his own admission, he struggled with self-control, having got used to always using violence. At the height of his career he would buy a different Ducati every week, and end every night drinking Cristal in nightclubs.

Undeterred, I asked him why Spain was so important to his clan. He told me that all the major Mafia families, not just the

Camorra, had had representatives living in the region for years. Their job was to deal with the brokers who supervised the shipments of cocaine arriving from South America. The Spanish Atlantic coast is one of the closest entry points into Europe for container ships travelling from Colombia. It was these giant vessels that had replaced the planes and high-speed boats that the cartels had used to supply cocaine to North America. Francesco's clan, the Camorra, had not only had a permanent Mafia cell in Spain, he admitted to me that he too had been directly involved in transporting drugs from Spain back to Naples. The clan had a team of mechanics who worked for them, and they would supply specially modified cars for the job. Aged just 18, Francesco drove one of these cars, fitted out with hidden compartments, from Naples to Spain. It was his first major drugs run for the Camorra. He was given simple instructions. He was to drive to a specific house, and just leave the car there. Then go off and act like a tourist, enjoying his time in Spain as if nothing was going on. A few days later he would return to his car and drive off. He would never meet anyone, but he knew that they had filled every one of the secret compartments in the vehicle with cocaine. This insulation protected each member, each link in the chain, from discovery. He couldn't tell the police who had stuffed the car with drugs even if he wanted to. Francesco would drive 250 kilograms (500 if he was working with someone else so they could take two cars) of virtually pure Colombian cocaine back to Naples. These loads could be sold back in Naples for up to 80 million lire per kilo. Meaning each one of these carloads had a street value of up to £15 million.

Francesco was a vital part of the cocaine pipeline I was following that linked the Cali Cartel with Spain and with the Italian Mafia. But did he have any information that would reveal how the Mafia might have got Colombian cocaine into Britain? I asked him if he knew of anyone from his family, from his clan, who had ever operated in the UK. It seemed I had yet again managed to find the perfect person to talk to. Francesco told me he had met with an English broker who had come to Naples from Spain to discuss a shipment of cocaine. I'd now found a direct link to Britain, but it sounded like it was British criminals in Spain, rather than Mafia operatives in the UK, who might be the crucial next stage in the process. Conscious he might have been risking his life talking to me, I shook Francesco's hand and wished him good luck.

I now knew I needed to find out who these British gangsters were who were orchestrating deals for Colombian cocaine with the Camorra in Spain. My next stop was Marbella. I was here to meet with Peter Walsh, a British investigator and author who specialized in British drug gangs. He told me how this part of Europe had enticed a certain breed of British gangster in their droves in the 1980s and '90s, to the extent that it had earned the nickname 'the Costa del Crime'. There was a very important reason for Spain's popularity with UK criminals – in 1978 the extradition treaty between Spain and the UK was annulled. This was a perhaps unforeseen side effect of the ongoing political clash between Spain and Britain over the ownership of Gibraltar.

Gibraltar is a British Overseas Territory at the very south of the Iberian Peninsula – giving its coastline and surrounding waters significant military and trade importance. Captured by the British in 1704, during the War of the Spanish Succession, it has been a bone of contention between the two nations ever since. Ceded, in perpetuity, to the British Crown by Spain in the 1713 Treaty of Utrecht, the Spanish nevertheless tried and failed twice to recapture it in the 18th century. Since the era of Franco, Spain has demanded the return of the territory. Britain, citing the majority opinion of the Gibraltarians themselves, who had rejected a possible joint-sovereignty agreement proposed by Spain and the United Kingdom, has refused to discuss the issue further with Spain without the assent of the local population of Gibraltar.

This ongoing political feud over 'The Rock', as Gibraltar is colloquially known, meant that the local authorities on the Costa del Sol had little or no interest in tracking down any of our hardened criminals hiding out in Spain, especially if they weren't overtly causing trouble on the costa. It was only a few brave British television presenters and reporters who were bothering to try to lift the lid on the gangsters sunning themselves by the sea and evading justice back home. In Peter's words, the UK mobsters in the millionaires' playground of Marbella were 'on the run, but they weren't running'.

But, as he told me, these were not minor players, these were 'the heavy mob. Serious armed robbers who had made their money "on the pavement", as they say in British cities – London, Manchester, Liverpool, Glasgow – in the '70s.' It was a veritable rogues' gallery.

Charlie Wilson, a key member of the infamous gang that perpetrated what became known as The Great Train Robbery, was there. In 1963 he had been a founding member of the gang who had taken £2.61 million from a Royal Mail train en route from Glasgow to London. He had been the gang's treasurer, responsible for divvying up and doling out each man's share of the loot. Captured soon after the robbery, at his trial he had refused to say anything at all – and had been dubbed 'the silent man'. He was sentenced to 30 years, but quickly escaped from HMP Winson Green and fled with his family to Quebec in Canada. After evading the authorities for four years he was finally tracked down when his wife called her family back in the UK. He was captured, returned to the UK and served ten years at HMP Durham. It was after his release in 1978 that Wilson moved to Marbella in Spain, where he was rumoured to have been involved not only in drug smuggling but also potentially in attempting to launder some of the £26 million proceeds of the infamous 1983 Brink's-Mat heist perpetrated at Heathrow Airport, the so-called 'crime of the century'.

So too was infamous nightclub owner Ronnie Knight. Knight had been friendly with the Kray twins in London in the 1960s, and had made his money from a pair of Soho clubs, the Artists & Repertoire Club (the A&R) and Tin Pan Alley, which were frequented by London's criminal fraternity. He fled to Spain in 1984, on the night of his brother John's arrest for his involvement in the 1983 armed robbery of the Security Express depot in Shoreditch, East London – in which £6 million was taken. Ronnie might have been safe on the Costa del Crime but, back home in England, his brothers John and James were both facing long stretches in prison for their respective roles in the heist.

Others with links to Spain in the early 1980s, when extradition was off the table, included regular holidaymaker and Billy Hill and Richardson gang enforcer 'Mad' Frankie Fraser. Gordon Goody, one of Charlie Wilson's pals from the Great Train Robbery, was out there running a beach bar. Kenneth Noye and John 'Goldfinger' Palmer – both linked to the Brink's-Mat heist – also attempted to evade British justice in Spain.

Safe in the sun of southern Spain, with no extradition to worry about, the British mob would bring their families out to visit and holiday with them. They'd party at the beach or host raucous, extravagant barbecues. But while these guys were happy to be away from the British police, and glad to be ignored by the Spanish authorities, they weren't ready to retire just yet. Ronnie Knight may have had his own Indian restaurant Mumtaz, and his club R Knights to keep him entertained, but for many of his generation of British gangsters on the costa a quiet life in the sun just wasn't enough. These were criminals at heart, and they had lavish lifestyles to maintain.

As we walked through the pretty paved streets of Marbella town, Peter explained how, as they cast around for a new, criminal source of significant income, this group of hardened British criminals found their attentions focused on the drug trade. Cocaine had been widely available in places like Marbella since the early 1980s. But these Brits abroad wouldn't have been able to procure the drugs directly themselves. They would have needed local partners to connect them with this supply from South America. And so the British expat criminal community found themselves dealing with the likes of Francesco and the Camorra who were already experts in smuggling drugs into Europe through Spain. Great Train Robber Charlie Wilson and many other infamous British gangsters elbowed their way into the Cali Cartel and Italian Mafia cocaine pipeline. For a few years they made hay while the sun shone, making millions in their new role as the British brokers arranging for Colombian cocaine to make its way to the UK. But their time in the sun was not to last for long. Soon a new generation of hungrier and even more violent British gangster was to arrive. The writing was on the wall for the old guard. Ronnie Knight, his cash running out, returned to Britain in 1994 to face justice. He plead guilty to handling stolen bank notes totalling over £300,000, just a fraction of the £6 million in cash that was taken from the 1983 armed robbery at the Shoreditch Security Express depot, but denied involvement in the robbery itself. He served three years of a seven-year sentence before he was released on parole. He lived out the rest of his life in Cambridge, far from the sunshine of the Costa del Crime, and died from pneumonia in 2023 after an ongoing battle with Parkinson's disease.

The new breed of Costa criminals arrived on the scene in Spain in the late 1990s. They were young and ruthless criminals who knew they faced sentences of up to 30 years if they were caught, and were prepared to do anything to protect their enterprise, and themselves. The prize on offer, the money to be made from the Spanish drugs trade, was so great that they didn't care who they had to take on.

Funnily enough, a big part of the appeal of the Costa del Sol to gangsters from all over the world – not the extradition status of Spain but the 'sol' part – was conspicuous by its absence for the other interview we filmed with Peter. We had travelled right to the Atlantic coast, to Galicia, famous for its smuggling operations – effectively the 'Spanish Cornwall', so he could show us the rugged coastline where ships from Colombia had once offloaded their cocaine for it to be smuggled into Spain. But on arrival we were greeted with a truly biblical downpour. Torrential rain was not something we'd really figured into our filming plan on the Costa del Sol. We did our best to shelter under some trees and ride it out, but when it became clear the rain was not going to stop any time soon we just had to wait for it to ease off and then make the best of it. By the end of that interview with Peter we were all soaked to the bone.

To better understand this bloody changing of the guard on the Costa del Crime, I got back in my car to drive to a rendezvous with one of this next generation of British criminals. In a quiet café with colourful prints on the wall, I sat down opposite Stephen Mee, a former drug smuggler. Unlike the old-timers who had initially been using Marbella as a sunny bolthole when things had got too hot in the UK, Stephen and his ilk 'weren't messing about. We knew what we was doing, we wasn't going there to party, we were going there to smuggle cocaine.' Stephen had once been number two on Interpol's 'most wanted' list, and was twice jailed for smuggling huge quantities of drugs.

In the mid-1990s he had served seven years in a Dutch Triple-A category prison for his part in a major cocaine deal with Colombia's infamous Cali Cartel. And immediately after his release and return to the UK, he served over 16 years of a 22-year sentence dating back to 1993 – for attempting to smuggle Colombian cocaine through the Dutch Caribbean island of Curacao. That sentence had been given to him *in absentia* – as he had absconded from police custody, escaping from a prison van on his way to Manchester Crown Court.

But Stephen's links to Spain went back to the 1980s, when he had been stealing high-end cars in the UK – Porsches, Ferraris, Rolls-Royces – and swapping them for cannabis in Spain. He'd get perhaps 50 kilograms of cannabis for a Rolls-Royce. But, as cocaine became more accessible with the opening of Cali's new trade route, he was able to move across to coke – which was easier to hide, easier to transport and ultimately far more profitable.

I asked Stephen if he had come into contact with Italian organized crime groups like the Camorra. I knew from my investigation so far that they were active in Spain, on the Costa del Sol and in Marbella, at the time. Stephen admitted they did indeed deal with Italians, but told me, 'I've never gone up to someone and asked them, "Are you in the Mafia?" ' But it made perfect sense to me when he said, 'When somebody's buying 200 kilos of cocaine it's not going to be Joe Bloggs.'

Stephen was already in Spain when, in 1987, he attempted his first cocaine 'smuggle'. He had flown out to Colombia, and travelled over the border to Ecuador – where much of the raw cocaine used by the Colombian cartels had initially been imported from in the early days. Here he purchased 24 kilograms of the white powder and filled a suitcase with it – as much as he could fit. He took the bag to the airport, dropped it off, and checked in on the same flight as a passenger. It was what he called a 'kamikaze'. Not least because at the other end of his journey, when he and the bag arrived in Europe, he didn't have an inside man to help him get the bag and its contraband contents safely through customs. He'd either get safely through or get caught. It was the luck of the draw. If he'd been stopped, and the contents of his bag discovered, he would have been looking at years behind bars. He was gambling his freedom on the promise of £60,000. But he got away with it. He started smuggling more and more cocaine, and dealing 20, 30, 40, 50 kilograms at a time. He was so successful that he became almost a one-man pipeline, long before the Cali Cartel formalized any deal with the Italian Mafia. Stephen told me that at one point the Colombians were dropping off loads of up to 1,000 kilos for him to distribute. His method for getting the cocaine into Europe was very similar to what would soon be adopted on an even bigger scale by Cali – containers on board international transport ships. He would have the drugs mixed in with a variety of items – one of his personal favourites was automobile engine blocks.

Stephen's operation grew so fast that he was soon one of the UK's most prolific cocaine traffickers. But it wasn't always plain sailing. When you're carrying £1 million to a drug deal with members of a Colombian cartel, things can easily go wrong. From what Stephen was saying, or not saying, it seemed clear he and his associates had been on the wrong end of a double-cross or two. But these brutal British gangsters wouldn't take being robbed of their cash lying down. I could see how in such circumstances any treachery could lead to bloodshed. Partners became rivals. Gang members became police informants. In the end, the authorities caught up with Stephen, and in 2004, after his release from prison in the Netherlands, he was finally made to serve time in the UK, for the crime for which he had been given a 22-year sentence more than a decade earlier.

I now knew that by the mid-1990s, with demand for cocaine at an all-time high, there were British gangsters, Italian mafiosi and Colombian cartels all combining to import cocaine from South America into Europe via the ports of southern Spain. But soon other criminal gangs were descending on Spain, keen to get a piece of the pie. Just as it had in New York and Miami, the importation and distribution hub for illegal drugs became a battleground. A brutal turf war broke out and the concerned Spanish authorities decided they needed to take action. They resolved to go up against the traffickers.

Leaving Stephen, I headed off to meet a former undercover police officer from the Spanish police. Over a coffee, Ricardo Toro, an ex-police superintendent who had been shot more than once and was a legend in the Spanish police, told me about his experiences going undercover to infiltrate the drug gangs of southern Spain. He and his colleagues would pose as drug buyers, convincing the suppliers that they were serious potential clients. It was dangerous work. Ricardo told me that one of his collaborators, a local Spanish woman, had been discovered. The gangsters didn't just kill her, they dismembered her body, chopping her up into tiny pieces.

I could see from his eyes that the memory hadn't left him even after all these years, that her fate still haunted him.

He remembered the war vividly, and tells me there were innumerable shootings and deaths right there on the Costa del Sol as British gangsters and Italian mafiosi fought over territory, took on their rivals or settled debts using violence and bloodshed. The warning signs had come as early as 1990, when Charlie Wilson, the Great Train Robber turned costa cocaine kingpin, was shot dead. A young man with a baseball cap pulled low to shield his eyes had knocked on the door of the Wilsons' Marbella home, and when wife Pat had answered he had asked, in a London accent, to speak to Charlie. She had showed him around to the back garden where the 57-year-old gangster was preparing a barbecue in celebration of the couple's 35th wedding anniversary. The young man spoke briefly with Wilson, then suddenly launched into an attack on him – kicking him in the groin, breaking his nose and then shooting him in the neck and head, before vaulting over the fence and fleeing in a van driven by an accomplice. Wilson's dog sustained a broken leg in attempting to defend his master and subsequently had to be put down. The murder was clearly a planned hit, and the suspicion was it was ordered by one of Wilson's criminal associates involved in the drugs trade.

Over the years, more and more gangland slayings would follow, reaching a brutal crescendo with two killings in 2002. First Irish gangster Michael McGuinness was found bound, gagged and very much dead in the boot of his own car at Malaga airport two days after he had been kidnapped at gunpoint. His hands and feet had been tied, and the corpse had already begun to give off enough of a smell to attract attention. Then Briton Scott Bradfield disappeared – only for his body to be discovered in two separate trunks found near Torremolinos. It seemed he might have been tortured before he had been killed and dismembered, and then his head, limbs and torso had been separated and placed in two identical pink Samsonite suitcases dumped in two different locations. One of them had been set on fire.

Soon the Spanish police had set up a special unit in the region to deal with the escalating violence. Ricardo was put in charge of this fledgling team, charged with just one objective – take down the cocaine traffickers by intercepting their supply routes. The man opposite me was the former leader of a unit whose sole purpose was to seize drug shipments coming into Europe. He told me that his biggest bust was of a 15,000 kilogram haul of cocaine, with a purity level of 97 per cent.

Ricardo and his team went after the Italian Mafia groups on the costa, primary among them the Camorra. The operation was a huge success, and I can sense his pride when he tells me that now, thanks to his efforts and those of his colleagues, 'the Camorra has fallen and has almost no presence in Spain'.

However, I knew that Spain, and the Costa del Sol in particular, was far from free of organized crime. The old-school British gangsters like Charlie Wilson might be long gone, and the Camorra might well have been chased out, but there was clearly a huge variety of organized crime groups from different countries across the world with a serious presence on the Costa del Crime. A gang war in 2020 had led to 20 murders in the Marbella area, and a dozen more in 2021. In fact, in 2024 local prosecutor Fernando Bentabol, who was taking on the drugs gangs in the province of Malaga, likened the situation in Marbella to that in Medellín, Colombia, during the violent reign of Pablo Escobar.

It was clear that the costa was still very much ground zero for the drug kingpins of Europe. Large numbers of gangs with links to Britain, Albania, Morocco, the Netherlands, Kosovo and Colombia had moved into the Malaga province, fighting for a slice of the lucrative drugs trade. Marbella, Puerto Banus and the surrounding region had become a key hub for an estimated 113 organized crime groups of 59 different nationalities, according to a report from the Spanish Intelligence Centre for Counter Terrorism.

Chapter Seventeen

Our Man in Rome

———

With my investigation in Spain at an end, I was casting around for a new lead. I was surprised at how many connections I had already uncovered between Britain and not only the Italian Mafia but also the American Mob, the Colombian cocaine cartels and even the ex-pat gangsters of the Costa del Crime – across a range of criminal activities from casinos to cocaine, murder to money laundering. It seemed impossible that the U K authorities didn't know more about the ongoing and evolving relationships between Britain and the Mafia.

Back in London I set about digging into the archives in a bid to uncover any evidence of past British attempts to document our connection to these global crime groups. Eventually I came across a story that soon had me packing my bags once again. It seemed that just over 30 years earlier the Italian government had themselves asked Scotland Yard for help. A detective had been dispatched to Rome, his brief: to work with the Italian authorities to investigate the alleged laundering of Mafia money through London. I discovered that this very detective was fortunately still alive, and eventually tracked him down. He agreed to come back to Rome to meet me.

On a roof terrace high above the street-level hustle and bustle of the Eternal City of Rome, Italy's historic capital, I met ex-Scotland Yard detective Gus Jones. Gus was a detective working in the organized crime division when, in 1990, he received a new posting. He was to be sent to Italy.

He told me that at that time the UK's knowledge of both Italian enforcement agencies and Italian organized crime was pretty minimal. However, he arrived in Rome having already previously met the country's leading anti-Mafia prosecutor, Giovanni Falcone. Together with his friend and fellow judge and prosecuting magistrate Paolo Borsellino, Falcone was at the forefront of the country's war against the Mafia. The pair had successfully taken on Sicily's infamous Cosa Nostra in the 1986–7 'Maxi Trial'.

Falcone and Borsellino were the flaming firebrands of the Italian justice system, the two men brave enough to take on the country's oldest Mafia. They were kindred spirits, and close friends. Falcone had been born in Palermo in 1939, Borsellino less than a year later – both in the same neighbourhood of Kalsa. As young boys they had played football together on the Piazza Magione. By the time they met again at Palermo University their political inclinations had polarized – but despite their differing world views, they shared one central and driving passion: a hatred of the Mafia. Falcone graduated from his law degree in 1961; Borsellino followed him a year later. Borsellino became a judge in 1963; Falcone in 1964 – having first practised law. Both worked in other parts of

Italy before Borsellino returned to Palermo in 1975 and then Falcone was appointed to the city's bankruptcy court in 1978. By 1980, as the violence known as the 'Years of Lead' raged around them, both men were embroiled in major cases against the Italian Mafia.

Falcone had joined the *Ufficio istruzione* (the Office of Instruction), which was the investigative branch of the Prosecution Office of Palermo. His new boss should have been Cesare Terranova, famous for prosecuting the Mafia in the 1960s – but he had been shot dead in late 1979. Terranova's replacement, Rocco Chinnici, soon put Falcone to work – prosecuting a case against the Sicilian Mafia, who were trafficking heroin to their relatives in New York City, the Gambino family. Three months after signing 55 arrest warrants related to the case, the Mafia found out it had been prosecuting judge Gaetano Costo who had dared to go against them. He was murdered, left bleeding to death on a Palermo pavement, and Falcone was immediately given personal bodyguards. Falcone soon pioneered a new way of building a case against the Mafia. Using techniques he had learned while investigating bankruptcies, he began to seize bank records and 'follow the money'. It was this approach that would lead to the discovery of the Pizza Connection.

Also in 1980, Borsellino had led a case that resulted in the arrest of six Mafia members. But before the end of the year the man with whom he worked most closely on it, Carabinieri captain Emanuele Basile, was shot repeatedly in the back while he carried his four-year-old daughter in his arms. Basile died of his wounds. His daughter miraculously survived unhurt. Borsellino was assigned to investigate the murder and, just like his friend Falcone, soon he too was deemed to require significant police protection.

As the 1980s progressed, and having seen their colleagues and friends gunned down, the men leading the fight against the Mafia in Palermo created an informal 'Antimafia Pool'. Falcone and Borsellino were two of the key figures in this group, who shared their intel and took collective responsibility for actions against the Mafia to give themselves greater protection. Then, in 1983, the founder of the group, Falcone's boss Rocco Chinnici, was killed by a car bomb. The device was detonated as he left his Palermo apartment to go to work – and the blast also killed his two bodyguards and the building's concierge. The 'Pool' were clearly getting too close to the Cosa Nostra. But, undeterred, these men of the law ploughed on – and laid the groundwork for their legal magnum opus, the Maxi Trial.

Combining their extensive investigations, the Antimafia Pool indicted 475 mafiosi for a multitude of Mafia-related crimes. The trial, held in a specially created courtroom, lasted from February 1986 until December 1987. Almost all of the accused were found guilty, and perhaps most importantly the legal process had now officially recognized the existence of the Cosa Nostra. This was due to the first ever testimony of a Sicilian Mafia boss turned pentito – Tommaso Buscetta – who told the court that the Sicilian Mafia was a single organization, headed by the *Cupola* (The Commission), the governing council of the various heads.

Gus told me that when he had met with Falcone he had discovered that the Italian was hot on the trail of Mafia money, and that the scent had led him to the UK. Gus had organized contacts for Falcone in the Channel Islands – and Guernsey, in particular. I could immediately see the link, these were tax havens. The perfect place to keep billions of lire of Mafia money being filtered through London. From what Gus was telling me it became clear that Falcone, and by extension the Italian authorities and state, had become aware of the connection between Mafia money made from drugs in Italy and laundering in the UK.

Gus went on to tell me that he later saw Falcone at a meeting in Rome, and went up to speak to him. What the man who was waging war on the Mafia told him had even the normally unruffled Gus concerned: 'The message is going out. I'm becoming too effective. I'm causing too much trouble. . . and my time is up.' It sounded like the last words of a man who knew he was about to die. And just two weeks later Gus's worst fear came to pass. . .

In March 1991 Falcone had moved to Rome, but had refused to give up his crusade against the Italian Mafia. Then, in January 1992, and in a huge blow to the Mafia, the Italian Supreme Court upheld the Maxi Trial convictions. It was decided that Falcone had to die. Not only that, but the Mafia wanted him killed in Palermo. They wanted to send a message.

On 23 May 1992, a car carrying Falcone, his wife Francesca Movillo and three police officers – Vito Schifani, Rocco Dicillo and Antonio Montinaro – was travelling along the A29 en route from Palermo airport to the couple's home in the city. As they passed over a culvert, 400 kilograms of explosives were detonated using a remote control by a member of the Sicilian Mafia stationed in an outbuilding on the hill overlooking that stretch of the motorway. The blast was allegedly so powerful it registered on local earthquake-monitoring devices. All five in the car were killed. It was a chilling echo of the fate of Falcone's friend, boss and the founder of the Antimafia Pool, Rocco Chinnici. Borsellino was having his hair cut when he heard about the explosion in Capaci and its apparent target, his childhood friend and fellow anti-Mafia campaigner Giovanni Falcone. Borsellino rushed to the hospital; but Falcone was dead.

Gus was by now painfully aware that the confidential report he had been working on, and that he had submitted before the firebrand prosecutor's assassination, touched on many of the same key issues which Falcone had been so aggressively prosecuting. Gus had submitted his findings to London in an extensive document officially titled 'The Mafia And Why It Matters To Us', which soon became known as 'The Rome Report'. Gus told me that one of the key findings from his work was that it was 'in the field of money laundering that the Italians believe we (the United Kingdom) have the most cause for concern'. The Rome Report flagged up for the UK authorities that Gus and his team believed huge revenues, generated by the illegal activities of the Italian Mafia, were passing through the UK, through London, and via 'offshore' accounts in places like the Channel Islands – and into UK properties and businesses. It seemed that the Mafia were not just washing their dirty money in Britain, they were then investing these newly laundered proceeds of crime into the country. Gus and his colleagues were hopeful that their efforts would raise awareness of the risks to the country as a result of the activities of Italian organized crime. Falcone's assassination made Gus even more certain that his report needed to be taken seriously and heeded urgently.

The Rome Report seemed like a smoking gun, allegedly containing the first documented evidence of Mafia dirty money successfully infiltrating Britain more than 30 years ago. To his knowledge the report went almost to the very top of the UK's political tree, and was seen by both the Home Secretary and the Foreign Secretary at the time. But, according to Gus, very few people seemed to take the findings seriously, and then – as now – the mention of the report or its findings would typically be met with a blank stare or the denial of any knowledge of it. Gus still had his own personal copy of the report, well thumbed and scattered with passages highlighted in pink or underlined in biro, but it is one of very few that remained. And yet, in his eyes, it was not only incredibly relevant and important at the time but was if anything even more so today.

And if the UK authorities failed to take The Rome Report seriously and neglected to take action in response to its findings, one organization certainly didn't: the Italian Mafia. The report was leaked to a newspaper, and Gus was named as one of its authors. Days later his 11-year-old son was leaving to go to school. Gus was surprised when the young boy came back upstairs clutching something to his chest. He opened his hand and there lying in his palm were three bullets. He had found them on the doorstep as he had stepped outside. It was an unmistakable message. The Joneses were a family of three. This was a bullet each for Gus, his wife and his son. Ignored in the UK, his Rome Report had clearly done more than just ruffle a few feathers in Italy; it had put him on the Mafia's radar. Gus never uncovered who exactly was responsible for leaving this chilling warning on his doorstep, but most likely it was the Cosa Nostra, who were the main focus not just of The Rome Report but also of the Maxi Trial and the attentions of Falcone and Borsellino.

On 19 July 1992, 57 days after the assassination of Giovanni Falcone, Paolo Borsellino was travelling with his police escort from his summer residence in the countryside outside Palermo back into the city to meet his mother. Just before 5pm the three cars pulled up outside the apartment block on the via D'Amelio where his mother lived. His escort didn't notice anything unusual, but, at 4:58pm, just as Borsellino walked over towards the entrance gate, 100 kilograms of TNT hidden in a parked (and recently stolen) orange Fiat 126 was allegedly detonated by Mafia trigger-man Giuseppe Graviano. The blast also caused the car that had been carrying Borsellino, and one of the two police escort vehicles, to explode. Borsellino was killed, as were five of the six police officers in his security detail: Agostino Catalano, Walter Eddie Cosina, Emanuela Loi, Vincenzo Li Muli and Claudio Traina. At the scene cars were on fire, and buildings were badly damaged or destroyed. The explosion was so powerful that human body parts were discovered up to four-storeys high on parts of the surrounding apartment blocks. In the aftermath of his friend Falcone's death, Borsellino had been systematically and compulsively recording all the links he and Falcone had uncovered between the Mafia and the upper echelons of Italian politics, business and power in a red notebook – his 'agenda rossa' – that he took with him everywhere. In the aftermath of the explosion, and the investigation, the notebook was never found. It remains the subject of conspiracy theories to this day. A major crackdown by the authorities following the murders of Borsellino and Falcone did at least lead to the capture of 'il capo dei capi' Salvatore Riina in 1993.

Falcone and Borsellino were both posthumously awarded the Gold Medal for Civil Valour, were acknowledged as martyrs of the Catholic Church and, in the 13 November 2006 issue of *Time* magazine, were named as heroes of the last 60 years. On the 30th anniversary of the deaths of the pair, Italy minted a special €2 coin in their honour.

They had been heroes of the fight against the Italian Mafia. But I was left in no doubt, knowing their fates and having heard of the message left on Gus's doorstep, of the very real risk to the life of anyone poking their nose into the business of the Cosa Nostra and their criminal associates.

Chapter Eighteen

The Port the Mafia Built

———

Before I left Italy behind, I had another key location to investigate. This was a place that, having seen the wild weather of the Spanish Atlantic coast and having heard about the crackdown on the Camorra and the smuggling of cocaine into Europe through Spanish ports, made perfect sense. I was off to find out more about an entry point for Colombian cocaine in Italy itself.

I drove south, towards the very tip of Italy's 'boot'. On the Calabrian coast I followed the signs to 'Gioia Tauro'. This state-of-the-art port was built in the mid-1990s – with Mafia cement, transported in Mafia trucks and poured by Mafia labourers. Its location was no accident – it's on the maritime trade corridor between the Suez Canal and Gibraltar, one of the busiest and most important shipping routes in the world. As a result it was now the biggest container port in Italy, and one of the top ten in all of Europe. I pulled into the car park for the Guardia di Finanza – the military police force that deals with financial crimes including tax evasion and money laundering as well as smuggling. Reporting directly to the Minister of Economy and Finance, the 'Financial

Police' has become the key agency tasked with suppressing the illegal drugs trade in Italy. It's a serious outfit: they have over 600 boats and ships and 100 aircraft, and not only patrol Italy's territorial waters but act as border patrol and customs at the country's airports.

I parked the hire car and entered the official-looking building to be greeted by Colonel Persano, the commander of the Gioia Tauro Financial Police. He was tall and impeccably dressed in his full uniform, and we shook hands beside the Italian flag. His welcome was a warm one, and he and his unit were keen to show me how they operated, so it wasn't long before I was back outside and part of a convoy of police vehicles, their lights flashing and sirens sounding as we arrived at one of the main container storage areas of the giant, sprawling port complex. I'd read a report that claimed that in the 1990s this port was controlled by the Mafia, at all levels. That meant the Italian Mafia had managed to create and control their own direct drugs pipeline from Colombia straight to Calabria. Even today, with the Mafia control of the port significantly diminished, as I stood on the dock with Colonel Persano's men, I could see the scale of the challenge that faced them. The containers, stacked one on top of the other, towered over us. The cocaine is smuggled in disguised shipments, hidden in seemingly random containers. Finding the drugs among the thousands of containers aboard the thousands of ships was like hunting for the proverbial needle in a haystack. And Colonel Persano told me that the Mafia continued to do their best to influence the workers in the port. Despite his best efforts it was almost certain they still had eyes and ears here – perhaps even today, as we were filming.

I was taken to a kind of semi-permanent portacabin set-up within the port, and here was greeted by customs officials. This was the scanning machine area, and the colonel told me that the team had a suspicious container that had arrived from South America that they wanted to take a closer look at. The official load had been listed as 'bananas' – but clearly the team were not convinced. He explained that bananas were a common cover for the importation of cocaine. Not only were they a major export for Colombia – the country was the world's fifth biggest exporter of the fruit, shipping over 100 million 20kg boxes every year – but they were also an almost identical density to cocaine. The cocaine packages were even shaped in the same way. As a result, loads of cocaine could be very effectively hidden within containers of bananas – as it can be very difficult even for the high-tech scanning apparatus the team were able to bring to bear to tell the difference. In this load, which they showed to me on the computer monitors on the desk, the final line on the scan, the last line of 'bananas' in the container, did not look quite the same as the others. It was hard to spot, but it was clearly a red flag. The colonel explained that it was possible that there were just a few blocks of cocaine hidden in that last line – and that this was a deliberate tactic used by the cartels and the Mafia to split up their shipments and reduce their risk. That way if drugs were discovered it was just one small part of the whole shipment – they were spreading their bets. Best estimates were that for every kilogram of cocaine Colonel Persano and his men found another

5 kilos could have been getting through. When he told me that they had seized over 35 tonnes of cocaine in two and a half years at this port alone I could see the scale of the operation. This was a tsunami of cocaine making landfall in Calabria, and while the Financial Police were intercepting huge quantities of it, my mind boggled at how much must have been sneaking through undetected and entering the Mafia's European distribution network.

The colonel took me out to observe his team as they started their inspection of the suspicious container. First, they used bolt cutters to cut through the thick wire looped around the bars that secure the container doors. Next, they inspected the tag on this seal, to ascertain whether it was genuine or a fake. A fake seal could have indicated that the container had been reopened after an initial inspection – meaning drugs or other contraband could have been hidden in it after it had been given the all-clear at its port of origin.

This time the tag seemed genuine, but that was no guarantee that there were no drugs inside. When the doors were opened up we were greeted by a floor-to-ceiling load of cardboard boxes of bananas. There were a lot of boxes, and a lot of bananas – and this was just one container. It was clear how much work the team had to put in in order to find perhaps just one load of cocaine. Millions of boxes of bananas just like these must enter this port every year – and we will probably never know how many of them actually contain drugs.

At least the Guardia di Finanza had money, resources and technology for their war on the drugs trade. The colonel's team fed a long wire inside the container. It was in fact a long, flexible fibre-optic camera. The wire was attached to a handset, on which a small display showed, in green and black 'night vision', what was within the deep, dark confines of the container. One man eased the flexible camera inside the container, threading it in, around and through the multitude of tightly packed boxes. Another kept a close eye on the handset screen, on the lookout for anything suspicious in the load or in the structure of the container itself. Smugglers sometimes constructed fake walls to smuggle contraband in sealed-off, hidden parts of a container. They also might stuff their illegal load within the structure of the container itself, inside its very walls. As the colonel told me, 'The only limit is their imagination. This is a challenge.' I could see it was one he relished, however.

The extensive survey of the container with the micro-cameras failed to turn up anything obviously suspicious. But the team were not ready to give up just yet. They brought another weapon from their arsenal to bear – a sniffer dog called Joel. Colonel Persano called him his 'best soldier'. Joel had been directly responsible for finding around 5 tonnes of cocaine in the previous two years. This was one talented canine.

It would take the team more than a day to complete their search of the container and its contents. I was unable to stay to find out if they did indeed discover that this was one of those being used to ship cocaine directly into Italy. But having seen how many containers arrived every day, and how long it could take to properly search just one, it was obvious that it was totally impractical, and impossible, to search every single one. It was an odds game, and one the Mafia were clearly willing and able to play. And it seemed to be worth it for them – it was estimated that 70,000 kilos of cocaine were smuggled through Gioia Tauro every year. This port was Europe's cocaine gateway – and the Italian Mafia, and many more of the continent's most powerful and influential organized crime gangs, appeared to have no intention of giving it up. I'd read a 2006 report that estimated that up to 80 per cent of all of the cocaine in Europe had arrived in Europe from Colombia at these very docks. I'd also heard that the Gambino crime family in New York had been exploring shipping cocaine and heroin to America from here in 2014. It seemed highly likely to me that a large proportion of the cocaine on the streets of Britain today had probably first arrived in Europe here, in Italy's far south.

Chapter Nineteen

The Lancashire Lass
Who Ran a Mafia Family

Back in the UK, I was on the lookout for any clues as to how the Italian Mafia had got their cash into Britain in order to launder it. A bizarre news story, about a British-Italian housewife in Lancashire, looked promising.

In 1994, not long after the publication of Gus's Rome Report and the assassinations of both Falcone and Borsellino, a mother of two living in the north-west of England was jailed for laundering illegal Mafia money. Her name was Marisa Merico, and I discovered that she was now out of prison. I tracked her down to an apartment block in Lancashire, and when I was able to get in touch with her she agreed to meet.

A drive back up north, and soon I was pressing the digital doorbell at the double doors of a charming mansion block. The woman who came down to let me in was as far from a Mafia crime boss as I could imagine – petite, blonde, dressed in a colourful print blouse, a silver crucifix hanging on a simple chain around her neck, and wearing a large pair of spectacles, her broad Lancashire accent and her whole appearance was more *Coronation Street* than *The Godfather*. Her unassuming home was absolutely spotless; it was like a show home. This was clearly a house-proud woman. But Marisa was the daughter of one of Italy's most notorious crime lords, Emilio Di Giovine.

Emilio was a Mafia godfather, the well-respected and feared boss of a Mafia family. Marisa's grandmother Maria, Emilio's mother, was known as *Nonna Eroina* (Granny Heroin), and had risen to such a position of power that she was in effect, if not necessarily in name, one of only a very few female Mafia bosses. She had married a tobacco smuggler and initially gained a reputation, and built a criminal empire, smuggling cigarettes. But, with the help of the criminal connections her sons had developed from their own stolen car enterprise, the family were soon able to upgrade from dealing in illegal tobacco to trafficking drugs – including hashish, cocaine, ecstasy and heroin – and guns. Together Maria and her son Emilio had risen to become the leaders of one of the richest and most powerful Milan Mafia families thanks to the success of their drugs trafficking operation, using Emilio's stolen cars to transport their product.

Over what else but a cup of tea, Marisa told me her extraordinary family story. Her mother Patricia was from Blackpool, Lancashire, a northern girl who went out to Italy to be an au pair. There she met Emilio, and in 1970 the couple had a daughter – Marisa. Eventually the couple split, but managed to stay on good terms, and their separation led to Marisa leading a bizarre double life, her time divided between Lancashire and Milan.

When I made a passing comment, remarking on how nice her home was, she began to reflect on how lucky she felt to be there – not just in this comfortable home in the UK but in fact alive at all. She told me there had been many dangerous times in her life, especially when she got married. Apparently at her wedding they had spotted two motorbike riders loitering near by – they were Mafia men, tasked with carrying out a hit on her dad. Luckily they decided not to go through with the assassination attempt. As she told me, 'it could have been a bloodbath, my wedding'. Not only that, she was three months pregnant at the time.

When Marisa ushered me into her living room, who should be on the sofa, engrossed in the bright screen of his mobile phone, none other but her father – the former Mafia don Emilio Di Giovine. Having served a significant portion of his life sentences, and survived the plots to kill him, Emilio had been released from prison and retired from his former life as a Mafia godfather. He stood to greet me, putting away his mobile as his daughter admonished him. Slight, and perhaps past his physical prime, Emilio was nevertheless very smartly dressed in a dark blue suit, white shirt and red tie, and something about him oozed a happy energy, a sort of joy that was forever on the point of breaking out in the form of a broad grin across his freshly shaved face. He was dapper, if no longer a don, but I could see an echo of the handsome young man who Marisa's mother had fallen for all those years ago.

Emilio, now working as a chef back home in Italy, had flown over to the UK to visit his daughter – and to meet with me. They told me that, as the daughter of a major Mafia boss, Marisa had been treated differently. She was his princess, and to touch her was to touch him. I could tell that it would take an exceptionally brave or foolish man to go anywhere near Don Di Giovine's daughter. This was a man who had commanded exceptional respect, most likely fear, throughout his Mafia family and beyond. Emilio explained to me how, when you are a Mafia family, everybody becomes mafiosi. Everyone is in it together. It was not just Emilio and his mother, but also his sister – and his daughter Marisa.

In 1987, at the age of just 17, Marisa moved to Italy – to join the family business. Sitting on the sofa beside her dad, she told me how she had become involved 'little by little'. She was particularly useful to the clan for her British passport and clean criminal record. An innocent-looking teenage girl from Lancashire, she was able to get through airport security without any problems. I asked her what exactly she had started out doing in service of the clan. She revealed that she had been used to transport large amounts of cash to pay for the shipments of cannabis – and her secret weapon was her underwear. Right there and then she produced a pair of 'big knickers, Bridget Jones's knickers', and, using bundles of paper to simulate rolls of cash, she showed me how she would layer them around herself, tucked into her pants, hidden beneath her clothes. She told me she thought she probably transported £150,000 or more at a time – and never got stopped, never ever got looked at. She was the perfect money mule, above suspicion, and a valuable asset for the family business. Emilio told me he was making two million a week. I guessed he meant pounds. Marisa interjected to explain that they were supplying nine countries. The pair were a fascinating couple – a proud father and loving daughter yet also professional criminals adept at smuggling drugs and money across international borders.

I was curious as to what they had done with the proceeds of their criminal enterprise; it's no mean feat laundering the kind of cash Emilio was talking about. Interestingly they told me that it wasn't through the UK that they had laundered their profits, but through Switzerland – where an accountant in Zurich had helped them funnel their money into banks and businesses, and even made them shareholders in a waterworks and a leather factory. I knew that Switzerland was known to be a good place to put your money if you wanted to keep it private – but I also wondered if another reason for not keeping their cash in the UK was its proximity to Marisa. Perhaps it was safer to have the cash abroad, rather than in one of the family's 'home' countries?

In 1992, when her dad Emilio was arrested and given two life sentences for his crimes, Marisa was expected to step up and lead one of the most dangerous crime families in Europe at the age of just 22. Marisa had the trust of her father. As he told me, 'she my voice'. She would visit him in prison every weekend, and he would pass notes to her in secret that she would then pass on to his men. Thanks to her efforts, the organization continued to run for another year. But then her aunt turned pentito – informing on her own family. She gave the police the names of the key members of the clan – and 300 people, her son and mother included, were rounded up and arrested. Three generations of Mafia family were destroyed.

Marisa, by now a mother, got her young daughter out of Italy, transferred nearly half a million pounds to the UK (which she would use to buy herself a fully furnished show home) and fled to England, leaving her life in Italy behind. Or so she thought. About a year later there was a loud knock at her door. It was a team from HM Customs and Excise. They searched the house, arrested Marisa, took her to a police station in Blackpool and eventually she was taken to HMP Durham. She was convicted of money laundering and sentenced to three years and nine months. Having got away with transporting Mafia cash into the UK as part of her family's multi-million-pound drugs business for years, Marisa had finally been caught and prosecuted – for effectively laundering illegal money through her otherwise legitimate investment in a family home for her and her daughter. Her escape plan had ultimately, and accidentally, led to her capture. HMP Durham was a top-security Category A prison. As a result, Marisa was now doing hard time alongside some of Britain's most notorious female criminals. For the crime of buying a house for her and her daughter with Mafia money, Marisa found herself rubbing shoulders, and sharing a shower block, with the likes of Myra Hindley – the 'most evil woman in Britain', who, together with lover Ian Brady, had between 1963 and 1965 perpetrated the 'Moors murders', killing five children and burying the bodies on Saddleworth Moor – and

Rose West, the serial killer who with her husband Fred murdered at least nine young women between 1973 and 1987.

But worse was to come. On her release from prison in Durham she was immediately extradited to Italy and sentenced to ten years, reduced to six for time already served in the UK.

Looking at her, it all seemed so hard to reconcile with the woman before me. I asked her if, when she looked back on it now, it was like looking back on someone else's life. She answered in the affirmative, going on to say, 'You're living your life looking behind you all the time. . . I'm a strong woman; I'm a survivor, I guess.' She has not only survived, but clearly found a way to start again, and to reinvent herself. As has her father. He told me that he had changed his life completely, that in 1992 he became a chef – and since then has worked with the police. 'I'm happy now. I know this life is bullshit. I'm really changed now.'

But it was made clear just how connected Emilio had been in his old life when, as we prepared to leave, he smiled another one of his warm, cheeky grins and handed over a folded piece of paper to the director. He told her it was the name of a killer. A man he had known in prison. A man intimately connected with Michele Sindona.

The mention of that name brought me almost full circle. Sindona was – just like Roberto Calvi, aka God's Banker, the man whose murder had started my entire investigation – an Italian banker with links to the Mafia, the Vatican and even Propaganda Due (P2). In fact, he was effectively Calvi's predecessor: known as 'The Shark', he had been the original 'God's Banker' – he had paved the way and even helped bring Calvi into the fold.

Born in Sicily in 1920, Sindona had obtained a degree in law in 1942 – having worked as a typist and bookkeeper's assistant from the age of 14 to pay his way through his school studies thanks to a scholarship, and then funding his time at university through working in the tax office and offering private tuition in physics and philosophy. Somewhat portentously his thesis was on none other than Machiavelli. But as the Second World War raged he found himself helping the Italian Mafia to smuggle food. These contacts meant that come the end of the war he was able to make a small fortune dealing in contraband on the black market – he even appears to have forged a transatlantic relationship with Meyer Lansky, the US Mob's 'accountant', who would tip him off as to where he could make the biggest profits. Then Sindona moved to Milan, set up his own accountancy firm and gained a reputation for helping big businesses and rich individuals avoid taxation by routing money through Switzerland and Lichtenstein. It wasn't long before Lansky and the US Mob called in their favour. Sindona was summoned to New York, and met with the Gambino family. Eventually he was entrusted with the important job of laundering the profits from their lucrative heroin business. At the same time he began to purchase banks. Over the next decade or so he amassed a significant collection of different Italian banks, and allegedly became a billionaire before he turned 30. From 1969 he began to route money from his banks through the Vatican Bank and on to a number of Swiss banks. In 1972 he even purchased a controlling interest in the Franklin National Bank in Long Island, New York. He was hailed as the 'saviour of the lira' and named 'man of the year' in 1974 by the US Ambassador to Italy, John A. Volpe. But three months later, in April 1974, there was a sudden stock market crash. Sindona had over-speculated and was dangerously leveraged. The crash led to what was dubbed *Il Crack Sindona* – The Sindona Bankruptcy. The Franklin Bank saw a 98 per cent drop in profits. Sindona lost $40 million. He began to siphon cash out of the Franklin Bank to try to prop up his crumbling Italian banking empire. When the Franklin Bank was declared insolvent it was discovered that Sindona had transferred $300 million to Europe in his failed bid to keep afloat.

While the collapse of the Franklin Bank was being investigated in New York, closer to home the Italian authorities had appointed lawyer Giorgio Ambrosoli to oversee the liquidation of Sindona's failed Banca Privata Italiana. Soon Ambrosoli found evidence of criminal acts by Sindona – including those involving the Franklin National Bank – and shared his findings with the US Justice Department. He had also uncovered supposed evidence that linked Sindona not only with Paul Casimir Marcinkus of the Vatican Bank but also with Banco Ambrosiano and its chief – none other than Roberto Calvi.

On 11 July 1979, just hours after speaking to colleagues in the US, Ambrosoli was dead. It was the evening of a major boxing match, and Ambrosoli had invited some friends to his house in via Morozzo della Rocca to watch it. He drove them home then, back at his own house, as he gets out of his car he hears someone calling him 'lawyer Ambrosoli'. When he responds in the affirmative the man utters the phrase 'excuse me lawyer' and fires four shots from a 357 Magnum at him. It is believed the man who gunned down Ambrosoli outside his home in Milan was one of a team of three Mafia hitmen. In the days before his death Ambrosoli had learned of evidence that purported to show how Sindona had been laundering the Mafia's heroin profits through the Vatican Bank and on to his Amincor Bank in Switzerland. The man who had uncovered this paper trail, Palermo Police chief Boris Giuliano, was shot and killed by the Mafia just ten days after Ambrosoli's murder.

In 1980 Manhattan's federal court convicted Sindona on 65 charges, including fraud, perjury and embezzlement, and he was sentenced to 25 years in US federal prison and fined $250,000. In a desperate attempt to somehow escape the US sentence, Sindona went to extreme lengths, even faking his own kidnapping (allegedly with help from friends in the Mob) and allowing himself to be shot in the leg to try to make the phony abduction appear as real as possible. His efforts failed, and he had endured a gunshot wound for nothing. In September 1984 an Italian request for his extradition was granted, so that he could face justice for the murder of Ambrosoli. While awaiting the culmination of that murder trial, Sindona was sentenced to 12 years for the fraudulent bankruptcy of the Banca Privata Italiana and given another hefty fine. Then, finally, on 18 March 1986, he was sentenced to life in prison for commissioning the murder of Giorgio Ambrosoli.

Two days after this last sentence was passed down, while being held at a prison in Voghera, in Lombardy, Sindona himself was in a coma. He had drunk a coffee containing potassium cyanide. He died two days later in Voghera's hospital. It was presumed he had sneaked the cyanide into prison, and had committed suicide when he had learned he would never be released. But this piece of paper from Emilio had me questioning that assumption. Had he really been murdered? And if so, by whom? Was it all to cover up his links to the Mafia, Propaganda Due and the Vatican Bank – and to the other man who I knew was also inextricably linked to those same three organizations, Roberto Calvi?

I waited until we'd left Marisa's pristine home before I took out the neatly folded square of white paper. Was this the moment I had been waiting for? This name might help me come closer than anyone ever had to truly solving the murder of God's Banker. This could be the perfect ending for my investigation and for the series.

I unfolded the paper. On it, written in Emilio's flamboyant, flowing cursive, were just two words: 'William Arico'. But who was Arico? And what did he have to do with Sindona and Calvi? I started digging to find out, and what I discovered did not disappoint.

On Sunday 19 February 1984, 47-year-old William Joseph Arico, a Long Island native, a convicted bank robber and a member of the Lucchese crime family, was being held in the Metropolitan Correction Center in Lower Manhattan, New York. He was in prison serving a four-year sentence for making a false statement – but the Department of Justice were attempting to secure his extradition to Italy. Italian police wanted Arico in connection with the assassination of Ambrosoli in Milan in 1979. They believed he had been paid between $40,000 and $50,000 by fellow New Yorker Robert Venetucci – the middleman in the deal – to carry out the hit on the orders of none other than Michele Sindona. Arico's extradition hearing had been scheduled for Tuesday 21 February, in two days' time.

On the Sunday night, Arico and his cellmate Miguel Sepulveda were back in their dormitory-style shared room in the high-security section of the federal prison. The 39-year-old Sepulveda was doing a 27-year stretch on a narcotics conviction. When things quietened down for the night the pair put their escape plan into action. Arico had previous – he had successfully escaped from Rikers Island prison in 1980, while awaiting trial for taking part in an attempted $2 million armed robbery of a downtown jewellery company – by swimming across the bay to Manhattan! By 8:20pm they had finished cutting through the bars of their cell window with a small saw – likely a hacksaw or jeweller's saw that they must have had smuggled into the prison. Next, they broke the glass of the window with a section of pipe.

As I read various reports of what happened next it started to get more than a little confusing. It seemed that soon they were climbing up the side of the building onto the roof above. However, no sooner had they got up there than they somehow found themselves surrounded by both police and prison guards. At least that's what one newspaper report seemed to claim. It made me wonder how the police and guards had discovered the escape and got there so quickly. Then, in attempting to get down to a lower roof using their homemade 'rope', it seems the bedsheets became untied and both men fell around 40 feet – from the ninth floor of the twelve-storey building to the fourth. Arico died in the fall. Sepulveda was critically injured and was taken to Bellevue Hospital. After that, it was hard to find out what might have become of him. I discovered that the Metropolitan Correction Center had only been built in 1975 and was designed to be escape-proof – but even by the time of Arico's failed bid it had already seen a litany of escapes, both successful and fatally flawed like this one. Many of them were almost identical in their methods. Years later a famous temporary inmate would be Gambino family crime boss John Gotti.

Interestingly, when Sindona was successfully prosecuted for the murder of Ambrosoli the authorities were able to produce a signed confession from William Arico, confirming that he had carried out the hit for Sindona. The authorities also had evidence provided by one of their most celebrated criminal informants, Henry Hill. Hill claimed Arico, a man he had met in around 1977 while the pair were incarcerated in Lewisburg prison – alongside none other than Robert Venetucci – and with whom he had partnered with on drug deals in the past, had told him he had carried out a hit for Sindona; that he had killed Ambrosoli.

Henry Hill Jr. had become an associate of the Lucchese crime family in New York in 1955 when he was barely a teenager. He was a hard worker and generally liked and trusted – but his Irish ancestry meant that, despite his mother's Sicilian origins, he was ineligible to become a 'made man'. He became part of the crew run by Paul Vario, a caporegime in the Lucchese family – and picked back up with his criminal colleagues even after a three-year stint at Fort Bragg in North Carolina, serving with the 82nd Airborne Division of the United States Army. He was involved in the 1967 Air France robbery at J F K International Airport, and his intel helped to formulate the plan for the famous Lufthansa heist at the same location some 11 years later. In the years in-between, the nightspot he purchased on Queens Boulevard, The Suite, became a regular Lucchese and Gambino crew hangout. He took part in the murder of Gambino family member William 'Billy Batts' Bentvena and he served four years of a ten-year sentence for extortion. He also began to deal drugs – something the Lucchese family forbade due to the lengthy sentences that it could lead to and the increased likelihood of those who were caught informing on their friends in return for leniency. It was at this time that he likely was working with William Arico – the name on my piece of paper.

As it turns out, the Lucchese family were right to be fearful – because in 1980 Hill was arrested on a drugs trafficking charge. He was soon convinced that Paul Vario, or those close to him, wanted him 'whacked' – for dealing in drugs contrary to family orders or to stop him ratting them out. Having narrowly dodged what he was sure was a plan to have him killed, when he was arrested for his part in the Lufthansa heist Hill did just what the Lucchese family had feared – he turned informant. His testimony resulted in 50 convictions, including against Paul Vario. Hill entered witness protection with his family. In 2012, in a Los Angeles hospital, he died from complications related to heart disease aged 69.

At the time of Arico's death in 1984 the Italian authorities requesting his extradition had already amassed a significant dossier of information linking him to Michele Sindona, and to Giorgio Ambrosoli's death. Key to this was an event that took place on 23 March 1981 – while Arico was on the run having escaped from Rikers Island and before his 1982 arrest. A man driving across the border from Canada into America was stopped at a border post in Vermont. He was found to be guilty of a minor currency violation, gave the name 'Ruzzo' and was quickly released on bail. But, as analysis of the documents confiscated from him would later reveal, this was none other than William Arico. His photo adorned a passport in the equally false name of 'Robert McGovern'. It contained numerous stamps from trips to Italy made between 1978 and 1981. They also found a leaflet from a Milan hotel, a diary, a handwritten note on a sheet of paper that referenced three banks in the centre of Milan, Robert Venetucci's business card with his phone numbers handwritten on the back, and Swiss bank account documents in the name of Robert McGovern. When they finally got hold of photocopies of these documents from their counterparts in the US, these details helped the Italian authorities piece together Arico's movements, often undertaken as McGovern – not least his trip to Milan between 8 and 12 July 1979 which coincided perfectly with the timing of the murder of Giorgio Ambrosoli on the night of the 11th. He had stayed at the Hotel Splendido during this visit, as McGovern, but had rented a red Fiat 127 under his Arico name. Witnesses would later claim to have seen the man who killed Ambrosoli leave the scene in a red Fiat 127. On 12 July 1979 'Robert McGovern' flew from Milan-Malpensa back to the Kennedy airport in New York.

Back in Lancashire, Emilio's handwritten note, pointing me to William Arico, did make we wonder if that man's death could have been very convenient for Sindona and for those powerful and shadowy entities associated with him. If he had confessed to US investigators, why was he trying to escape? Did he fear for his life if he was sent back to Italy? Should he have been worried about his safety even while in prison in America? The authorities had ruled his death an accident during the failed prison escape – but had there been more to it than that? I had also heard rumours that Arico's confession might have implicated one or more senior political figures in Italy. Was his death, potentially like that of Sindona himself in prison in 1986 and Calvi in London in 1982, all part of those closest to them cleaning house – making sure that the financial crimes committed by both of 'God's Bankers' on their behalf did not get linked back to them? It certainly seemed very convenient that Calvi, Arico and then Sindona had all died in mysterious circumstances just at the moment the noose was tightening around them. If you wanted to make sure they didn't flip – and do a deal with the authorities – then the only way to be certain was to silence them for good. Was this what had happened to one or two – or even all three – of them?

That evening, back in the hotel, I reflected on everything I had learned from Marisa and Emilio, and throughout my journey to uncover the hidden links between Britain and the Mafia. A journey across the globe that had taken in the US Mob, the Colombian cocaine cartels, British gangsters on the Costa del Crime and much more. And a journey that had, surprisingly, taken me to Preston.

Twice. It seemed surreal. Even more so when, having a nightcap with the crew before our trip back down south the next day, we found ourselves surrounded by Italians in the hotel bar. I think we all took a double take. I had spent weeks finding out just how widespread Mafia influence was, and how they had clearly infiltrated Britain and been here for decades. Surely this was a coincidence? We finished our drinks, and went to bed. The Italians stayed in the bar drinking.

Chapter Twenty

A Very 21st-Century Mafia

———

Having met Marisa and Emilio I now knew that England had been the home of a senior family member of a very active Mafia clan. But the pair were long since retired from their past lives of organized crime, it seemed. In my investigation into the links between Britain and the Mafia I had uncovered a huge range of intersections between organized crime and the UK – a Mafia banker murdered by Mafia operatives in London, one of the killers then himself taken out on British soil; a Neapolitan Camorra hitman hiding out in Preston while scamming credit cards and popping back to Naples to murder his clan's rivals; a Mafia don running a restaurant empire and laundering money in Aberdeen; British East End gangsters – including the Krays – partnering with the US Mob in London casinos; our role in supplying the bootleg whiskey that empowered the Italian-American crime syndicates in the United States during Prohibition; Mafia operatives in the UK helping Britain's biggest cocaine kingpin import his drugs from Colombia; and Brit gangsters muscling in on the Cali Cartel and Italian Mafia's cocaine pipeline to Europe on the Costa del Crime. It was clear that our relationship with the Mafia – whether it was the original Italian families and clans like the Cosa Nostra and Camorra or the 20th-century US Mob – went back almost a hundred years, had ebbed and flowed and changed over time, and had been more wide-ranging than I could ever have expected.

But our modern world had never stopped evolving – and neither had the nature of organized crime. From bootleg alcohol during Prohibition to gambling and then to drugs – cannabis first, then heroin and cocaine – the Mafia in Italy and beyond had always not only moved with the times but had stayed one step ahead of the game – and the authorities. And today, that was as much the case as ever.

The Mafia, in the end, were all about money. They wanted to make the most cash possible, while taking the least possible risk. Just as they moved from gambling to drugs because they could make more profit, or from cannabis to cocaine because it was easier to hide and transport – and far more lucrative – so, as the 21st century progressed, they had moved further and further away from the physical transportation of narcotics and embraced our civilization's new 'Wild West': the internet. The digital age, and in particular the changes that have occurred with the invention of the World Wide Web, had presented the ever-ingenious Mafia with new opportunities to make billions. With the advent of online banking, and the creation of cryptocurrencies like Bitcoin, came new, quicker, safer, more anonymous ways to move, hide and launder their vast criminal wealth. No more Bridget Jones's knickers stuffed with cash. And the exponential growth of the online marketplace – from banking to shopping – had also facilitated the invention of new digital crimes. The Mafia were expanding into hacking, phishing and other digital criminal activity and moving gradually away from their historical areas of expertise such as racketeering, extortion, gambling or drugs. And often using experienced cyber-criminal partners, hiding behind masked IP addresses and anonymous identities, they had never been safer.

In 2015 European police agencies uncovered a major credit card hacking operation, led by hackers based in Russia, Ukraine and Romania, and targeted at stealing the credit card details of mostly American citizens; it was being run by a crime ring based on the Italian island of Sicily. The gang had links to the Cosa Nostra.

In 2021 Europol and the Italian and Spanish national police forces carried out a major raid as part of a year-long operation code-named 'Fontana-Almabahia'. The criminal enterprise they were targeting was based on the Canary Island of Tenerife, part of Spain – where the police had been tracking the activities of a newly arrived cohort of Italian mafiosi. In the operation 16 houses were raided and 106 arrests made. The majority of those involved were Italian, and many had links to the Mafia – including the Neapolitan Mafia, the Camorra.

The suspects defrauded hundreds of victims using phishing attacks and other types of online fraud such as SIM swapping – in which criminals convince phone service providers to transfer victims' phone numbers to another device to access accounts – and infiltrating business emails. The victims – the majority of them

Italian, but also Spanish, English, German and Irish citizens – were convinced into arranging bank transfers of thousands of euros at a time to Spanish accounts controlled by the gang. The cash, estimated at €10 million a year, was laundered through a wide network of money mules and shell companies. The authorities froze 118 bank accounts and seized hundreds of credit cards, SIM cards, POS (point of sale) terminals and other electronic devices.

Europol found that the network was well organized, with individuals each having their own specific areas of responsibility. The gang included computer experts, who created the phishing domains and carried out the cyber fraud – including phishing and vishing (voice phishing, using phone calls) attacks and the use of social engineering techniques to gain access to individuals' banking credentials; recruiters and organizers in charge of the money muling; and money laundering experts, including experts in cryptocurrencies.

The stolen money was laundered through online cryptocurrency purchases or ploughed back into other, more traditionally mafiosi criminal activities, such as prostitution, drug production and trafficking, and arms trafficking.

It was clear that cybercrime and hacking, traditionally the domain of Russian criminals and Nigerian gangs, was very much part of the Italian Mafia's 21st-century criminal menu. However, this Italian-led gang hadn't forgone all the old ways. They had also been employing some of their more 'old school' tried and tested techniques. Several of those arrested were also accused of kidnapping, assault, coercion, robbery with violence and force, illegal possession of weapons, and even two counts of homicide. One case involved mobsters kidnapping a woman and taking her to a cash machine at gunpoint, forcing her to withdraw all of her money.

It seemed the Mafia were pioneering a new form of blended crime, combining an expansion into cybercrime with their more traditional methods of making and laundering money. And whether they were based in Italy, Spain or even on the Canary Islands, modern technology and criminal methods meant anyone anywhere in the world – including back in the UK – could be an accomplice, or could be a victim.

This move seemed to have gathered pace. Just 17 people were murdered in Mafia-linked killings in Italy in 2022. In 1991 the number had stood at 700. The mobsters had instead targeted the low-risk area of white-collar crime – pivoting to tax evasion, and to financial fraud targeting national post-COVID recovery funds, home improvement schemes and even a European Union stimulus package worth €200 billion. In 2023, almost a third of the cases being investigated by the European Public Prosecutor's Office (EPPO) – which investigates crimes against the financial interests of the European Union – were focused on Italy. The value of these Italian cases was estimated at nearly €7.5 billion.

The rewards for the criminals were obvious. And these were also low-risk crimes compared to those more traditionally carried out by the Mafia. Selling as little as 50 grams of cocaine could land you in jail for up to 20 years. But filing false invoices to defraud the government of €500 million in tax credits would only result in somewhere between eighteen months and six years in prison. These new crimes were lower risk, and higher reward – and it was inevitable that the Italian Mafia would not take long to get involved.

I had followed the trail of the Mafia from the 1982 murder of God's Banker under Blackfriars Bridge in London to a Lancashire caravan park, an Italian restaurant in Aberdeen, London's casino scene in the Swinging Sixties, the mean streets of New York and Philadelphia, the rise and fall of Atlantic City, the battle for Miami, the Cali Cartel in Colombia, the Costa del Crime, Rome and Naples and then finally, and improbably, back to Lancashire. I'd uncovered a catalogue of crimes linking not just the Italian Mafia but also their American cousins, the US Mob, to Britain. And I'd discovered how Colombian drug lords and East End gangsters had all played a part in the criminal networks and international pipelines that linked the UK to the Mafia. It was clear these links had existed for decades, from Prohibition in the 1920s to the present day, from illegal liquor, via gambling and drugs, to the most modern criminal enterprises of all – hacking and cybercrimes. The links between Britain and the Mafia were long, complex, fascinating – and, it seemed, far from dead. And my investigation had been one of the most intriguing and memorable of my career. But, after all that digging, hours and hours of research and calls, all those days of travelling, walking the streets of Philly, hiking the Colombia hills in body armour, and meeting some of the most feared, menacing and charismatic men in the history of organized crime, I felt like maybe, just maybe, I'd earned a rest. Just for a bit!

Acknowledgements

Based on the TV Series *Ross Kemp: Mafia and Britain* on Sky HISTORY.

Editors for Sky HISTORY:
Dan Korn
Di Carter

Editors for Honey Bee:
Ed Taylor
Ros Edwards

Editor for Freshwater Films:
Ross Kemp

With thanks to:
David Arrowsmith, Sarah Bishop Fenn, Trevor Davies, Anabel Fairclough, Scarlet Furness, Phelan Glen, Emma Lyons, Hana Mallett and Alex Segal at InterTalent Group,

Charlotte Robertson, Sam Taplin, Elaine Wong, and the team at Sky HISTORY.

sky H | HISTORY

Acknowledgements for David Arrowsmith:
I'd like to thank those that have supported me throughout the process of working on this book – my family (especially my wife Irma), my agent Charlotte Robertson, the team at Octopus Books (not least Trevor Davies and Scarlet Furness), Ed Taylor and Ros Edwards at Honey Bee, and the one and only Ross Kemp himself of course.

Index

About the Author

———

Ross Kemp is a BAFTA award-winning documentary maker, actor and television presenter. Ross has built a reputation as one of the most exciting and hard-hitting documentary makers in the industry. His fearless investigative work has garnered international recognition, shining a light on some of the world's most dangerous and complex issues. From war zones to organized crime, Ross has also authored 12 books, which have sold over half a million copies worldwide.

Picture Credits

Inside:

Getty Images/Bettmann 99, New York Daily News Archive 128

Plate section:

Alamy Stock Photo: Colaimages 1a, Jack Kanthal/Associated Press 3b, Nati Harnik/Associated Press 4a, Remo Nassi/Associated Press 2a, Trinity Mirror/Mirrorpix 3a; Getty Images: Bettmann 5b, Express/Hulton Archive 2b, Robert Rosamilio/New York Daily News Archive 6a; © Honey Bee, Group M Motion Entertainment, Freshwater Films: 1b, 4b, 5a, 6b, 7a, 7b, 8b; Shutterstock: News Group 8a.